SPECIAL OLYMPICS

INSTRUCTIONAL MANUAL

...FROM BEGINNERS TO CHAMPIONS

Julian U. Stein, *Consultant*
Programs for the Handicapped, AAHPERD

Lowell A. Klappholz, *Publisher*
Physical Education Newsletter
Old Saybrook, Connecticut

Published Jointly

by the

AMERICAN ALLIANCE FOR HEALTH,
PHYSICAL EDUCATION, RECREATION
AND DANCE
1900 Association Drive
Reston, VA 22091

and

THE JOSEPH P. KENNEDY, JR. FOUNDATION
1701 K Street, N.W.
Washington, D.C. 20006

Foreword

In 1968 the Kennedy Foundation and the Chicago Park District tried an experiment. We organized a national sports competition for the mentally retarded, called it the Special Olympics, and invited participation from all over the country.

Many experts said it was doomed to fail. Retarded children, they said, could never run 300 yards, swim the length of a pool, or travel by airplane a thousand miles from their homes or institutions.

But, as the opening parade went by that July day at Soldiers Field, we knew beyond a shadow of a doubt that the experts were wrong.

There were floor hockey players from Canada in their bright uniforms. Dozens of athletes from almost every state in the union. As they marched past the reviewing stand, they heard the bands playing and parents and friends cheering just for them for the first time in their lives.

And once the games began, they displayed a spirit of courage and determination that overcame all the labels, all the obstacles the world has imposed on these children.

Since 1968 the Special Olympics has grown beyond our dreams. All 50 states and the District of Columbia now have Special Olympics meets, and Puerto Rico, Canada and France are deeply committed to the Special Olympics program.

Why is it that 100,000 volunteers and 325,000 mentally retarded youngsters are deeply, whole-heartedly involved in this program?

Why is it that dozens of distinguished athletes are helping to train the Special Olympics athletes and lead sports clinics?

I think it's because Special Olympics has taught us all something very precious. In an age of super-professionalism and commercialism in athletics, the Special Olympics reminds us of the true meaning of sportsmanship, character, courage and competition.

These boys and girls run and jump and swim out of the sheer joy of exercise. They love the crowds, the cheers and the medals—but more than anything, they love the chance to play. And isn't play what athletics is really all about?

In our competitive society, we've learned to value the strong, the quick and the successful. The Special Olympics teaches us that there are other qualities to be prized in athletics as well. Qualities of courage and generosity that these special children have in rare abundance.

I can never forget the crippled boy who ran his race on crutches. The blind boy who followed the voice of his coach down the track. The little girl who stopped at the finish line to wait for a friend. The young man who loved running so much that he didn't stop at the finish line but tried to run another lap around the track.

And I can never forget the parents and friends who hugged their children as they crossed the finish line no matter where they placed. Feeling pride in their achievement, perhaps for the first time in their lives.

The Special Olympics Games provide never-to-be forgotten memories for all who participate. But the heart of the Special Olympics is not the local or national games. It is the day-by-day chance the special child gets to exercise, play, join in team sports, swim, learn skills, share in all the joyful experiences that are so essential for all children. It is here that the child learns the *worth* of accomplishment that helps him in school, in work, in his future life.

But to do this, the child must have the help of parents, teachers, teenage volunteers, physical educators and sports specialists.

This manual was commissioned by the Kennedy Foundation to provide a handbook for volunteers who want to organize games, team sports and recreation for special children on a year-round basis. These programs can be conducted at institutions, schools, day camps, municipal playgrounds and swimming pools, everywhere there is room to run or jump or throw a ball.

We dedicate this manual to all volunteers who will make parents proud of their children, and children proud of themselves.

Eunice Kennedy Shriver

Eunice Kennedy Shriver
President
Special Olympics, Inc.

iii

A Word About Competition

Competition, like play, progresses through definite and identifiable stages in which a youngster strives to attain a goal that is *important to him*. He—

- *Competes* with himself to improve his own performance as he tries to do more sit-ups or push-ups, jump rope longer, or throw a ball higher into the air and catch it.

- *Competes* with himself against his own best performances as he tries to run the 50 yard dash or swim the 25 yard freestyle faster, jump higher or further, or throw a softball further.

- *Tries* to attain specific goals to receive a medal, certificate, patch, ribbon, points, other recognition, or the personal satisfaction that comes from success.

- *Cooperates* with others to achieve a mutual goal such as winning a relay, simple game, or lead-up activity.

- *Competes* with others to win a position on a team or a place in a group in which only a certain number can participate and/or compete against other teams or groups.

Individual and group competition parallel individual and group play. Since Special Olympics events are mostly individual in nature, they provide youngsters with individual challenges and the inner satisfaction of success and accomplishment. This motivates each competitor to try harder to do better as he strives to improve his previous best performances.

Help each youngster learn to play hard and compete to the fullest so as to create a success cycle and overcome the pattern of failure and frustration that often plagues retarded youngsters who have not had opportunities to play, participate, compete, and achieve. One successful experience usually leads to other achievements which in turn help to develop self-confidence and the belief that "I can" and "I will" rather than "I can't" and "I won't."

It is important to tell youngsters that they may do their best to win—practice hard all season, take part in every workout, and run or swim as fast as they can in competition—and still not come in first. When they understand this, they have won a victory for themselves, over themselves—although someone else finished first, the Special Olympics has become a truly educational and lasting experience. Do not insult their intelligence by telling them they've won when it is obvious they haven't!

When retarded youngsters become active participants, tryers, and doers rather than passive spectators, sitters, and watchers, they've started to develop confidence which leads to success in all walks of life—constructive competition contributes mightily to participation, achievement, and victory.

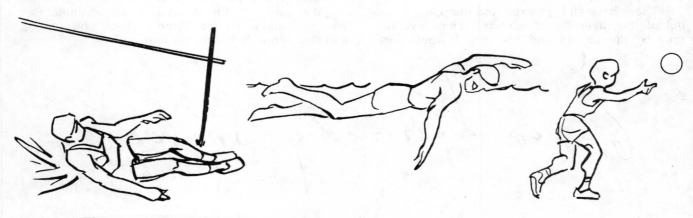

Table of Contents

iii   **Foreword**

iv   **A Word About Competition**

vi   **A Special Note to Special Olympics Coaches and Organizers**

1   **To the Coach**

Where You Come In 1
The Special Olympics—What It Is 1
A Coaching Guide for You 2
You and Those You Coach 3
Values of Sports 3
What You Gain From the Program 4
Safety 4
On the Field of Play 4
What It's All About 4
Teaching and Coaching Tips 5
Selected Basic References 5

6   **Fitness and Conditioning**

Special Olympics Workout Sheet 8
Conditioning and Fitness Cycles 9
Bending/Stretching 10
Flexibility 12
Muscular Endurance: Arms and Shoulders 15
Abdominal Endurance 18
Balance 21
Power/Speed 24
Agility 27
Coordination 29
Cardiorespiratory Endurance 33
Team Log Activities 36
Resistance Activities (Weight Training) 38
Chair Activities 39
Confidence Courses 40
Conditioning/Fitness References 40

41   **Track and Field**

Guide to Special Olympics Performances 42
Using Track and Field Cycles 44
Cycles 1-10 45
Flexible Five 64
Running Form 65
Running Drills and Practice Activities 69
Track Special Fundamentals and Teaching Activities 72
Guide for Timing Interval, Rhythm and Pace Workouts 74
One Mile Run 75
440 Yard Relay 78
Jumping: Standing Long Jump and Running High Jump 81
Softball Throw 89
Pentathlon 94
Selected Track and Field References 94

97   **Volleyball**

Cycles 1-10 98
Volleyball Fundamentals 106
Selected Volleyball References 109

110   **Swimming**

Practice Cycles 110
Landlubber's Loosen-Up—Warm-up 111
Five Fathoms—Conditioning 112
Cycles 1-10 114
Crawl Stroke Fundamentals and Teaching Progressions 119
Backstroke Fundamentals and Teaching Progressions 123
Swimming in Lanes 128
Interval Training 128
Freestyle Tactics and Teaching Progressions 129
Circuit Training 130
Relay Fundamentals and Teaching Progressions 134
Backstroke Fundamentals and Teaching Progressions 135
Nonstop Rhythmical Aquatic Routines 136
Fun Activities 137
Selected Swimming References 138

A SPECIAL NOTE
TO
SPECIAL OLYMPICS
COACHES AND ORGANIZERS

Activities described in this manual are not suited for every retarded child and adult. The retarded display such a wide range and variety of abilities and limitations that understanding and discretion are required in designing individual and group programs.

Therefore, it is strongly recommended that you recruit professional guidance and supervision. The Special Olympics *coaching staff* will probably always be comprised mainly of individuals with limited knowledge of exercise and sport—teachers, parents, high school and college students, businessmen, and other volunteers. However, they should have the benefit of advice and assistance from a trained professional in physical education or sport. He can provide direction and control in planning and conducting your Special Olympics training program to insure a happy, healthful, productive and safe learning experience for all your young *athletes*.

As with any sport program, every participant should have a medical examination prior to participation in training or competition. This has been a problem in many communities but now hundreds of doctors across the United States have volunteered their services as Special Olympics team doctors and as Medical Directors for Special Olympics Games. They provide assurance that the participants are physically and emotionally ready for the Special Olympics experience and prescribe the special care and precautions necessary for some children. They also insure that training and competition are conducted in a safe and healthful environment.

For assistance, we suggest that you contact your city or county medical association or the local chapter of the American Academy of Pediatrics.

To the Coach

In the past seven or eight years, physical educators, recreators, coaches, and classroom teachers have joined forces to increase educational, recreational, and sports opportunities for mentally retarded youngsters and adults. These efforts have been aided tremendously by volunteers—parents, high school and college students, community leaders, and *others like you* have become actively involved in helping the retarded succeed and *become more independent while having fun*. Most volunteers have been exceedingly successful in working with and coaching retarded youngsters in sports, games, and similar fun activities. Many programs and opportunities for retarded could not have been attempted, much less continued, without the dedication and unselfish contributions of volunteers of all ages.

In recent years, teachers, coaches, and other leaders have learned that—

- Mentally retarded boys and girls can succeed, even excell, in sports and games.

- Volunteers can coach and work successfully with retarded youngsters.

- Competition can spur retarded youngsters to undreamed of achievement.

- Success can enhance self-image and self-discipline of mentally retarded.

- Achievement in play and sports can provide the retarded with self-confidence needed to stimulate achievement in other aspects of life.

- Individuals with learning problems can profit substantially from participating in sports, physical fitness, and recreational activities—accomplishments and positive attitudes developed on the playing field can affect performances in the home, in the classroom, and on the job.

- Mentally retarded individuals are more like their nonretarded peers than they are different. They respond effectively to methods, activities, and procedures that have been successful with the nonretarded. While intellectual and academic differences between retarded and nonretarded cannot be overlooked, activities and approaches used most successfully with mentally retarded reflect likenesses—not differences—with good, logical, sequential physical activity programs.

WHERE YOU COME IN

As a volunteer in the Special Olympics program you will work with individuals to help them become physically fit, to inspire them with the desire to compete, achieve, and lead more meaningful lives as a result of acquiring skills in a variety of activities and through taking part in sports.

You will not be alone in this endeavor. You can get help, direction, and assistance from coaches, physical education teachers, and recreation specialists in your community. Ask them to hold clinics for you, to suggest appropriate materials and resources, and to help you in your coaching assignments. They can provide you with the know-how for success. Some may even spend a practice session with you and the youngsters.

THE SPECIAL OLYMPICS—WHAT IT IS

The Special Olympics were organized in 1968 by The Joseph P. Kennedy Jr. Foundation to provide mentally retarded youth eight and over with opportunities to participate in a variety of sports and games on local, state, regional, national, and international levels.

Special Olympics programs are not intended to take the place of physical education and recreation programs now being conducted in schools, communities, day care centers, and residential facilities. They are not designed to serve as a complete physical education or sports training program. Basic objectives are to—

- Encourage development of comprehensive physical education and recreation programs for mentally retarded in schools, day care centers, and residential facilities *in every community*.

- Prepare the retarded for sports competition—particularly where no opportunities and programs now exist.

1

- Supplement existing activities and programs in schools, communities, day care centers, and residential facilities.
- Provide training for volunteer coaches to enable them to work with youngsters in physical fitness, recreation, and sports activities.

It's important that youngsters participate in well-rounded physical education programs all year long. *It is not enough to train them only in Special Olympics activities for a few weeks and consider the job done.* Youngsters need lots of opportunities to run, jump, swim, and throw—they learn to move and then move to learn.

Early in the school year concentrate on a variety of activities such as soccer, football, tag, racing, jumping, jogging, tumbling, and gymnastics; for some, the entire emphasis may be on simple-fun games. As time for Special Olympics in your community draws near, place greater emphasis on Special Olympics events. Encourage all to participate and prepare for competition; guide youngsters into activities they enjoy the most along with those in which they have had greatest success. Organize regular classes like team practices with different teaching and coaching stations for various events. In track, for example, have stations for running, jumping, throwing, and practicing the relay. Circulate and observe youngsters—hopefully you'll have an assistant or two to help so each station is well supervised; use capable youngsters as event leaders or station assistants. When Special Olympics are over, return to the comprehensive program. If operating strictly an out-of-school program, start preparing specifically for Special Olympics early in the year.

Within the present framework of the Special Olympics program—track and field, swimming, gymnastics, floor hockey, and volleyball—volunteer coaches can plan a wide variety of physical education, recreation, and sports activities to keep kids fit and to change the pace of formal practice. Other activities that motivate youngsters to participate and succeed include:

Competition with other groups.

Field trips to see local teams play.

Outings and picnics.

Hiking and cycling.

Movies of athletes and games.

Speakers such as outstanding local athletes or coaches.

A COACHING GUIDE FOR YOU

This manual has been prepared to help you work with youngsters. It contains sections on general conditioning and fitness as well as separate sections on track and field, swimming, and volleyball. Each section provides helpful information on fundamentals, form, and conditioning for specific events, teaching activities and progressions, preparing for competition, and strategy; lesson cycles are guides for planning and conducting practice sessions.

This *Special Olympics Instructional Manual* is all that volunteers and others with little background or experience in physical education or athletics need to conduct a Special Olympics program. However, greater understanding of activities, methods, and cycles results from planned inservice programs for persons working with youngsters in the Special Olympics program. Inservice sessions can include—

How to work with retarded boys and girls

How to use the manual and cycles.

Opportunities to try different activities and methods outlined in cycles.

Films, talks, and demonstrations by local coaches and their teams, question and answer sessions, as well as instruction on using the manual are appropriate and helpful inservice activities and approaches.

Motivation and stimulation are essential to successful performance. In addition to motivational devices described in track and field (pp. 41 - 44), and swimming (p. 111) sections, try these approaches—

Set up special awards such as hardest worker, most improved, most courageous, best performer in each event in each age group.

Present medals, cards of merit, crests, certificates, ribbons, patches, and other special recognition at end of year, or at periodic desserts, parents days or nights, assemblies, demonstrations, or other special events.

Make a youngster want to participate and he will to the best of his ability. Setting realistic, meaningful, challenging, and attainable goals is important to the development of positive play and competitive practices.

Help youngsters set—

- Immediate goals for each workout or practice session.
- Intermediate goals for a week or month.
- Seasonal goals which can be revised if achieved ahead of schedule.

While keeping the eye on the ball is vital to hitting, shooting, and kicking, Frank Robinson, Kareem Jabbar, Tom Dempsey, and countless other successful athletes stress the *follow through*—the ability to finish a job. When you help a youngster set goals for every practice session, every week, every month, and every season, see that he keeps his eye on the ball and follows through. Work with youngsters to keep them running, jumping, and swimming toward *their* desired goals. Encourage them to stick to it and take pride in what they are doing. Praise them, encourage them, make them taste success.

YOU AND THOSE YOU COACH

In addition to learning to teach fitness activities and fundamental sports skills, develop a positive understanding of the mentally retarded. To succeed in working with the retarded and to provide them with opportunities through sports and games, you need to—

- Understand the problems of retardation and to accept and respect each retardate as an individual of worth and dignity.
- Establish rapport with individuals and the group as a whole.
- Plan and conduct comprehensive fitness, athletic, and recreation programs.
- Participate in training programs to increase understanding and appreciation of mentally retarded and to improve skill and competency in coaching specific Special Olympics events.
- Be flexible and able to change approaches to meet needs of individual youngsters—have the courage to make changes and adjustments to improve team and individual performances.

Many believe that the attention span of the mentally retarded is extremely short. It is true that some mentally retarded individuals do exhibit a short attention span, but this is often caused by disinterest, boredom, and lack of motivation and understanding—it is not an inherent or universal characteristic. When motivated and interested in an activity—when they can see progress in an activity that has meaning to them—many mentally retarded of all functional levels and ages show great patience and ability to stick to a task. Should attention wander and interest wane, change activities frequently and keep formal practice sessions short; approach the specific fundamentals and skills in a variety of ways with different activities.

Recognize that each youngster is an individual with different skills, ideas, attitudes, and interests. Work with each individual and strive to provide direction, leadership, and know-how for youngsters to achieve, succeed, and have fun. While respecting the rights of individuals, be firm and consistent in discipline. Purposeful activity is one of the best ways to avoid disciplinary problems—keep youngsters busy, happy, and playing hard and they will have neither time nor inclination to misbehave.

VALUES OF SPORTS

On the field of sport and in play are sown seeds of character and discipline so vital to an individual's future success and happiness. As youngsters learn skills of a sport, they also acquire habits and attitudes that may be more important to their future development than success on the field. They can learn to—

Win graciously and to lose gracefully—don't brag in victory or alibi in defeat.

Play the game hard in an effort to win—winning isn't everything but the desire to win is everything.

Be loyal to teammates, cooperative with coaches and officials, and courteous to teammates, coaches, officials, and opponents.

Respect those of different races or creeds.

Be considerate of those with less ability and respect those with more ability.

Develop self-discipline.

Suppress selfish desires for the good of the team.

Those who direct sports programs for American youth play a vital role in imparting these important lessons. Set an example by what you do as well as by what you say—kids would rather see a sermon than hear one; be active, workout with youngsters, and earn their respect. As you work with youngsters, set a good example—

Be a good sport and keep sight of the real goals of the Special Olympics program.

Treat each youngster fairly regardless of his athletic ability.

Be firm, understanding, kind, and patient—they make winning people.

Respect opponents and be a lady or gentleman at all times when talking with officials—be careful not to criticize officials or their decisions in front of participants.

Be the kind of coach for whom you would want your youngster to play.

Life's prizes are not won by those who are endowed with nature's gifts—they are won by those with a will to win.

WHAT YOU GAIN FROM THE PROGRAM

As you expend time, energy, and strength to help mentally retarded youngsters, you—

Derive the self-satisfaction that comes from helping youngsters develop physically, mentally, emotionally, and socially.

Realize what it means to contribute to society by using your time to help others in the community and by setting a positive example for others to emulate.

Learn to work with young people, their parents, officials, and volunteers, and acquire the experience and talent to get along with a variety of people of different ages, abilities, and interests.

Gain status in the community for services performed.

Participate in personal recreation that helps you grow physically, emotionally, and socially.

SAFETY

It's impossible to discuss all aspects of safety related to physical activities in general and Special Olympics in particular. Ask a local physical education teacher or recreation specialist to give you a list of appropriate safety rules and to spend some time with you talking about safety on the athletic field, in the gymnasium, and in the swimming pool. Here are some suggestions—

Keep playing areas free of clutter and debris.

Let youngsters have fun but let them know that you won't permit unsafe activity—*don't tolerate horseplay.*

Inspect facilities and equipment to see that they are safe.

Purchase good equipment—don't economize on equipment at the expense of youngsters.

Anticipate possible safety hazards and problem areas and take appropriate precautions to avoid them—*an ounce of prevention is worth a pound of cure!*

Make haste slowly—logical, sequential, and progressive procedures provide important safeguards in all physical education, recreation, and sport activities.

ON THE FIELD OF PLAY

Plan and organize practice sessions so little time is wasted. Know what you are going to do but be ready to adjust to situations that occur during practice sessions or due to weather conditions. Part of planning is to see that practice areas are lined or painted for play. Circles, squares, rectangles, or lines may be painted or marked on various playing surfaces. Use—

Circles for tag games, to teach youngsters to run around curves, and for volleyball drills involving passing, volleying, or serving.

Squares or rectangles for boundaries in games, as drill areas in volleyball, and for different running activities.

Lines placed 10, 20, or 30 yards apart for shuttle relays and activities, for starting and finishing races, and for learning to run in lanes.

Paint or draw circles, squares, or other shapes on walls for targets for throwing activities and volleyball drills. Prepare areas in advance to save time for practice, play, and competition.

WHAT IT'S ALL ABOUT

When all is said and done, you are participating in a program that has one purpose—*to provide mentally retarded youngsters with opportunities to succeed and accomplish through participation in broad based physical activity and recreation programs.* Within this framework, help each youngster develop—

- Self-respect, self-discipline, and self-confidence.
- Physical, social, emotional, and mental fitness.
- Positive values such as sportsmanship, responsibility to the team, and respect for others.
- The will to succeed.
- The ability to achieve to his maximum potential.

Be positive—there is no room for negative expectations when dealing with the mentally retarded. Show each youngster by your voice and actions that you have confidence in him and you *know* he can complete the task confronting him. A common error is the tendency to overcoach—don't fall into this trap. Teach one thing—*and one thing only*—at a time. There's no hurry; take lots of time to get youngsters into good shape and to teach them fundamentals. It is essential for every youngster to make gradual progress and know that he is improving. As you work with youngsters—

√ *Focus on ability*—not disability

√ *Emphasize potential*—not deficiency

√ *Encourage*—not discourage

√ *Accentuate the positive*—not the negative

√ Find a way for *every* boy and girl to succeed.

TEACHING AND COACHING TIPS

Keep all youngsters active.

Keep verbal directions simple and brief.

Demonstrate and participate—the retarded are great mimics and will follow your example.

Praise and encourage youngsters. Even if the attempt is unsuccessful, praise the effort and some part of the attempt that is done well. Be specific in praise—"nice serve," not "good boy."

Keep practice time on specific activities short. Performance may be best the first few times a skill is tried—shift activities often within a practice session.

Introduce new activities early in a practice session before youngsters get tired; vary the tempo of a workout to reduce the fatigue factor.

Be patient.

Use visual aids as supplementary coaching tools.

Review and repeat skills, drills, and games in many different ways.

Stimulate and motivate youngsters to succeed by using appropriate motivational devices.

Move an individual through a desired motion, movement, or skill such as the crawl or backstroke in swimming, throwing a softball, or the serve in volleyball—this is an excellent coaching device.

Coach to physical and intellectual levels of youngsters who are at different stages of development and skill. Recognize this, work with it, and be sensitive to each youngster's abilities, interests, and experience—use activities and approaches that are neither too difficult nor insult the intelligence of the individual.

Keep instruction slow, deliberate, sequential, and concrete—make haste slowly but surely.

Keep the fun in fundamentals. When youngsters enjoy what they're doing, they are more likely to participate and succeed. They'll all be champions in their own eyes—and in yours—when they are motivated to play and try again.

Select devices and methods that challenge youngsters with different abilities.

Be resourceful, have initiative, be imaginative; try new ways, modify old approaches, make equipment, and have the courage to experiment.

SELECTED BASIC REFERENCES

American Association for Health, Physical Education and Recreation. *The Best of Challenge.* Washington, D.C.: The Association (1201 16th St., N.W.), 1971.

American Association for Health, Physical Education and Recreation. *Recreation and Physical Activity for the Mentally Retarded.* Washington, D.C.: The Association (1201 16th St., N.W.), 1966.

American Association for Health, Physical Education and Recreation. *Physical Activities for the Mentally Retarded: Ideas for Instruction.* Washington, D.C.: The Association (1201 16th St., N.W.), 1968.

Athletic Institute. *The Volunteer Coach-Leader.* Chicago, Illinois: The Institute. (805 Merchandise Mart).

Klappholz, Lowell (Editor). *Physical Education for the Physically Handicapped and Mentally Retarded.* New London, Connecticut. Croft Educational Services (100 Garfield Ave.), 1969. Order from Physical Education Publications, P.O. Box 8, Old Saybrook, Connecticut 06475.

Fitness and Conditioning

Five fitness cycles have been designed to help mentally retarded boys and girls get into and retain good physical condition so they can experience success in and enjoy a variety of physical activities. *Rookie, winner, star, champ,* and *super champ* cycles reflect a youngster's status in each of nine fitness components:

1. *Bending and stretching*—move the trunk and upper body forward, backward, or sideward.

2. *Flexibility*—stretch front and back of thighs.

3. *Arm/shoulder endurance*—use arms and shoulders for longer periods of time.

4. *Abdominal endurance*—use abdominal muscles for longer periods of time.

5. *Balance*—maintain good posture and alignment of body parts while moving or not moving, in various positions, and on stationary or moving objects.

6. *Power/speed*—increase force and quickness of leg movements.

7. *Agility*—change direction of body movements.

8. *Coordination*—combine movements of different parts of the body into smooth, synchronized, and graceful patterns.

9. *Cardiorespiratory endurance*—increase the ability of the heart and lungs to sustain vigorous activity for longer periods of time.

The most balanced conditioning program is achieved by using one activity from each of the nine components every practice session. However, a balanced program can still be achieved by selecting activities from components 1-3-5-7-9 (as numbered above) one day, and from components 2-4-6-8-9 the next; continue in this alternate pattern. All activities can be selected from the same level—*rookie, winner, star, champ, super champ*—or from different levels for each component according to individual needs—*bending/stretching,* rookie; *flexibility,* winner; *muscular endurance,* super champ; *abdominal endurance,* star; *balance,* champ.

With some youngsters, especially young, timid, and inexperienced, it may be necessary to emphasize one or two components. Gradually, add activities from one or two other components as youngsters become more proficient in learning patterns and movements. Continue this process until one activity from each component is included in each practice. Each practice session should include a minimum of 10 minutes of conditioning activities.

Generally, if a youngster is unable to perform at least one activity from each component at the rookie level, schedule more fun activities of an informal nature rather than stressing the competitive aspects of Special Olympics. Work with coaches, teachers, and parents in other schools, residential facilities, day care centers, activity centers, or communities to arrange informal play or field days. These same activities can be a valuable supplement to regular Special Olympics programs by providing more and varied opportunities for all youngsters.

Variations have been provided for each activity to add interest, challenge, and variety to conditioning routines. Some variations are more difficult than the basic activity while others are less difficult. Variations are one more way to provide a gradual progression from level to level and to zero in on each child's needs. Each variation does one of the following:

- Changes the activity while retaining the basic position.

- Changes the basic position while retaining the activity.

- Changes both basic position and activity.

Catchy names have been given cycles and activities to create interest, attract attention, and motivate kids. Nothing is sacred about these names. Let youngsters develop their own names for cycles and activities.

Many basic activities and variations are self-testing and self-motivating. Youngsters can see their own progress when they can do an activity more times or do it faster. Motivate them even further with such approaches as:

"How many times can you push-up (sit-up) from when I say go until I say stop?" After a

6

brief rest challenge youngsters to do as many push-ups (sit-ups) in the same time. This illustrates an interesting and fun approach in which activity and rest are alternated in various combinations.

"Do 10 push-ups (sit-ups) as fast as you can." Time youngsters and after a brief rest see if they can do 10 push-ups (sit-ups) faster.

Keep personal records and squad charts to recognize success and progress and to show individual squad members how much they have improved in various activities.

Use individual workout sheets as a guide for recording progress and determining when a youngster is ready to try another variation or move to the next level. Encourage youngsters to take copies of workout sheets home as a guide to home conditioning on nonpractice days. A sample workout sheet is shown on the next page.

Music can be used in many ways—as background for activity, as a change of pace, for variety, and for basic activity. Often just the rhythm of music helps youngsters perform better. Bending and stretching activities are more fun done to records such as *Bunny Hop*. Records such as *Alphabet Song* (Golden Records LP 114, Affiliated Publishers, 630 Fifth Avenue, New York, New York 10020), *Physical Fitness for Pre-School and Kindergarten* (RRC 703, Rhythm Record Company, 9203 Nicholas Road, Oklahoma City, Oklahoma 73120), and *Chicken Fat* (CF 1000, Capitol Records) include many of the nine components and offer another fun way to fitness.

To help youngsters develop understanding and ability to perform, use any or all of the following teaching procedures:

Manual guidance—guide youngster through desired movements so that he gets the feel of the activity. For example, move a youngster's right hand to his left toe and his left hand to his right toe to do the windmill.

Tactile—touch body parts to be moved so the youngster *feels* what parts of the body to move in each activity. For example, touch his left toe and right hand to indicate parts he is to move in the windmill.

Sight—use demonstrations, pictures, films, slides, loop films, and other visual devices to show a youngster what he is to do. For example, have him perform the windmill with you. Imitation is a good way for youngsters to learn when they have good models.

Auditory—give verbal instructions or problems for youngster to solve. For example, ask him to do a windmill or if he can touch one hand to the opposite toe.

Signals—use signals, signs, words, numbers, colors, drum beats, or similar cues. For example, the word red, a single blast of a whistle, or two beats on a drum can mean, "do a windmill." This approach is fun for youngsters who have to be alert to look and listen for signals telling them when to start, stop, speed up, slow down, change directions, and so on. Let youngsters take turns giving signals.

How you use these lesson cycles and how long you spend on each cycle depends on each individual situation. Factors influencing use of cycles include ability of youngsters, number of participants, number of volunteers, and length and frequency of practice sessions. In the first practice session find out where all youngsters are in terms of physical condition—search for fitness levels in each component by:

Asking them to do simple activities in *rookie* and *winner* cycles.

Observing them in simple activities such as running, skipping, touching toes, or jumping up and down.

Watching them play simple games requiring them to perform movements used in conditioning and fitness cycles; play records and watch youngsters move in rhythm and perform activities in time with the records.

As you use the cycles the progression within each component will become obvious; *what a youngster learns as a rookie helps him to be a winner.* There is some relationship in learning and development between components in conditioning cycles. For example, simple windmill movements are made more complex in woodchopper; push-ups are added to squat thrust sequence. Change emphasis in a given exercise to stress different fitness components; learn movements and patterns in early cycles and use them for more difficult purposes in later cycles.

To use cycles effectively:

Be prepared to deal with individual strengths and weaknesses.

Emphasize areas of deficiency. If a youngster is having a particular problem in the area of flexibility or balance, stress these components in his conditioning program even if it means placing less emphasis on other aspects of the program, particularly his strong points.

Vary formal conditioning activities by using fun approaches suggested in cycles and incorporating other fun-type activities described following the lesson cycles.

SPECIAL OLYMPICS WORKOUT SHEET

Name _____ Date _____

Fitness Component	Coach/Teacher Instructions	Parent/Attendant Comments
Bending/ Stretching		
Flexibility		
Muscular Endurance		
Abdominal Endurance		
Balance		
Power/Speed		
Agility		
Coordination		
Cardiorespiratory Endurance		
General Suggestions		

HOW TO USE WORKOUT SHEET

Provide information to help and guide parents, ward attendants, cottage parents, big brothers, or youngster himself plan conditioning and fitness activities for fun and recreation.

Include information such as levels and names of exercises/activities, instructions, and hints for each exercise/activity including number of repetitions and/or sets, games, and fun activities that emphasize fitness components.

Provide additional information and comments to help persons who use this workout sheet concentrate on interests, needs, and abilities of youngster.

Take exercises/activities/variations from conditioning and fitness section, place information in appropriate spaces on this form, and send to person who is to work with youngster at home, on ward, or in cottage.

Include information for general workouts in which all fitness components are emphasized or to concentrate on weak or poor components in need of special attention.

Devise ways so youngster who cannot read can also use this workout sheet; drawings, stick figures, or other pictorial means can communicate what and how each exercise/activity is done.

Motivate youngster to participate at times other than in formal practice sessions by providing special rewards and recognition for home/ward/cottage workouts.

Help each youngster develop a positive attitude toward and love for participating regularly in vigorous physical activities.

Encourage persons working with youngster in home/ ward/cottage situation to send information about supplemental workouts including personal comments and observations, improvement and progress, questions, and suggestions.

Adapt or modify this form or develop one designed to meet specific needs of youngster. For example, eliminate names of fitness components on workout sheet and simply provide blocks to list activities and to record progress over a specified time period. Be sure time period workout sheet covers is short so changes in exercises/activities can be made as youngster improves, progresses, and has new needs. Consider reproducing workout sheets with rookie, winner, star, champ, and super champ exercises/activities. Although this approach does not provide the flexibility to individualize to meet youngster's needs, it is practical and a time saver.

Conditioning and fitness activities are fun and rewarding for youngsters. How well they succeed, how much fun they have, depends on you.

CONDITIONING AND FITNESS CYCLES

	ROOKIE	WINNER	STAR	CHAMP	SUPER CHAMP
1 Bending/ Stretching	Wing Stretcher	Body Bender	Trunk Twister	Wood Chopper	Standing Elbow Knee Touch
2 Flexibility	Touchdown	Windmill	Sitting Windmill	Sitting Crossover	Inverted Bridge/ Arch
3 Muscular-Endurance (Arms-Shoulders)	Support/Walk Activities	Modified Push-Ups	Push-Ups	Special Push-Ups	In-Orbit Push-Ups
4 Abdominal Endurance	See-Saw	Sit-Ups	Bent/Leg Sit-Ups	Curl	V-Up
5 Balance	Basic Body Balances	Balance In Motion	Stork Stand Progression	And Away We Go	Boards and Beams
6 Power/Speed	Vertical Jumps	Piston	Partner Push	Inverted Bicycle	Mountain Climber
7 Agility	Side Step	Shuttle Run	Dodging Run	Zig-Zag Run	Boomerang
8 Coordination	Jump and Turn	Jumping Jack	Sensational Seven	Squat Thrust Series	Astronaut Drills
9 Cardiorespiratory Endurance	Bench Step	The Runner	Crazy Legs	Run/Walk	Roadwork

NOTE: *A balanced program results from selecting one activity per practice session from each of the nine categories. However, a balanced program results from selecting activities from components 1-3-5-7-9 one day and 2-4-6-8-9 the next day, continuing in this alternate manner. All activities can be selected from the same level (rookie, winner, star, champ, super champ) or from different levels for each component according to individual ability and level* (bending/stretching, *rookie;* flexibility, *winner;* muscular endurance, *super champ;* abdominal endurance, *champ;* balance, *rookie). Supplement fitness, conditioning, and cycle activities by using confidence and obstacle courses, resistance or weight training, team log activities, and chair activities. Details and teaching suggestions can be found following cardiorespiratory activities, pp. 36 - 40, in this section.*

BENDING/STRETCHING
ROOKIE

Wing Stretcher

Stand erect, raise elbows to shoulder height, touching clenched fists in front of chest; keep palms down.

Thrust elbows backward vigorously and return.

Keep elbows parallel to floor.

Keep head erect.

Variations:

- Touch fingertips.
- Extend arms to side and back to front in opening and closing pattern.
- Change speed and vigorousness of movements.

Body Bender   **WINNER**

Stand with feet slightly apart.

Keep feet still, toes pointed straight ahead, head and eyes straight ahead

Bend backward as far as possible.

Return to starting position.

Bend forward as far as possible.

Return to starting position.

NOTE: Bend from hips so only upper body moves.

Bend left as far as possible.

Return to starting position.

Repeat pattern to right.

Variations:

- Clasp hands behind head on neck/on hips, or hold against legs.
- Place feet closer together or farther apart.
- Change speed and sequence of activity.

10

STAR

Trunk Twister

Stand with feet shoulder width apart, hands on hips.

Keep feet still, toes pointed straight ahead, head and eyes straight ahead.

Bend and twist left as far as possible; continue across front of body to right; continue twisting and arching backward to left.

Keep back parallel to floor while moving across in front of body.

Arch back when moving in backward direction.

Variations:

- Clasp hands on neck behind head.
- Place feet closer together or farther apart.
- Reverse direction so half of time is spent moving left to right and half right to left.
- Change speed of activity.

CHAMP

Wood Chopper

Stand with feet slightly more than shoulder width apart.

Grasp left thumb with right hand and rest both hands on right shoulder.

Variations:

- Change speed of activity.
- Place hands on hips; reach between legs, touching hands on floor as far behind heels as possible.

Swing arms vigorously to the left as if swinging an ax; bring hands down and as far back between legs as possible; bend knees to get hands further back on downward swing.

Return to standing position with hands on left shoulder.

Continue in alternate manner down between legs and return to opposite shoulder.

11

Standing Elbow Knee Touch

Stand with feet as far apart as possible.

Place hands behind head with fingers interlaced.

Bend forward at waist.

Touch both elbows to thighs (knees, ankles, toes, floor); keep knees straight.

Variations:

- Touch head and forearms to floor.
- Place feet closer together or farther apart.
- Touch alternately right elbow to left thigh (knee, ankle) and left elbow to right thigh (knee, ankle).

FLEXIBILITY
ROOKIE

Touchdown

Stand with feet comfortably apart.

Stretch hands and arms over head.

Bring arms down touching fingertips (knuckles, closed fists, palms) to thighs (knees, shins, ankles, toes, floor); keep legs straight.

Variations:
- Touch both hands in front of (outside of, inside of) right (left) foot.
- Move feet closer together.
- Stand on bench (curb of track, raised board, brick, cinder block) and bring fingertips as far below level of feet as possible.
- Hold beanbag in right (left) hand, drop it to side, and pick it up with left (right) hand.
  NOTE: Keep legs and arms straight.

Windmill

Stand with feet shoulder width apart, hands on hips.

Twist and bend the trunk, bringing right (left) hand to left (right) thigh (knee, shin, ankle, toe); keep arms and legs straight.

Return to starting position.

Continue alternating sides.

Variations:
- Extend arms sideward at shoulder level, palms down.
- Move feet closer together or farther apart.
- Touch floor as far outside of foot as possible.
- Touch floor behind heels.

Sitting Windmill

Sit with legs spread slightly more than shoulder width apart.

Place hands on hips.

Touch right (left) hand to left (right) thigh (knee, shin, ankle, toe); keep arms and legs straight.

Return to starting position.

Continue, alternating sides.

Variations:
- Extend arms sideward at shoulder level, palms down.
- Place hands behind head with fingers interlaced; touch elbows.
- Touch both hands to left (right) toe; hold chin (nose, chest) to knee (floor outside of knee); alternate sides.
- Grasp right (left) knee (calf, shin, ankle, toe) with both hands; hold chin (nose, forehead, chest) to knee (floor outside of knee, floor inside of knee); alternate sides.
- Move legs closer together or farther apart.

NOTE: Keep legs straight.

Sitting Crossover

Sit with legs spread as far apart as possible.

Place hands on floor outside of hips.

Keep left leg straight as it crosses over right leg; touch left heel outside of right ankle.

Return to starting position.

Continue, alternating sides.

Variations:

- Touch heel as far past ankle as possible.
- Touch toe instead of heel.
- Move hands further back from hips (lean on elbows).
- Lie flat on the back, extend arms straight to the side from shoulders, palms up—touch alternately right toe to left hand and left toe to right hand (see illustration below).
- Touch both legs together to right, then left.

> The credit belongs to the man who is actually in the arena, whose face is marred by dust and sweat, and blood, who knows the great enthusiasm, the great devotions, and spends himself in a worthy cause.
>
> Theodore Roosevelt

Inverted Bridge/Arch

Take position on back with knees bent and heels tight against buttocks.

Place hands on floor near ears with fingers spread and pointed forward (similar to back roll).

Keep elbows and arms parallel.

Lift stomach and arch body until arms and legs are as straight as possible—make a high bridge.

Hold for increasing lengths of time.

Variations:

- Move feet away from buttocks.
- Keep top of head in contact with floor.
- Continue in up and down pattern as a reverse push-up.
- Sit and place hands on floor outside of hips; keep legs straight—lift buttocks off floor as body is straightened and neck extended.

MUSCULAR ENDURANCE: ARMS AND SHOULDERS

Basic starting position for activities at all levels unless otherwise indicated:

Place palms of hands on floor just under and slightly outside of shoulders.

Point fingers forward.

Keep body straight.

Focus eyes slightly in front of hands.

Variations:

Use at all levels and with most activities.

- Move arms closer together or farther apart.
- Raise upper body by placing hands on a bench (seat of a chair, log, cinder block, partner's back).
- Raise legs by placing feet on a bench (seat of a chair, box, log, cinder block, partner's back).
- Use knuckles (closed fist, finger tips) instead of palms of hands.

Support/Walk Activities

Use basic starting position (p. 15)
unless otherwise indicated.

Straight Arm Support/Walk

- Support for five (10, 15, 20, 30) seconds.
- Keep feet in place—use hands to move body in circle around feet.

Bent Arm Support/Walk

- Bend elbows to approximately 90 degrees and support for five (10, 15, 20, 30) seconds.
- Keep feet in place—use hands to move body in circle around feet; keep elbows bent.

Coffee Grinder

- Support body on right arm and both feet; keep arms and legs fully extended with feet slightly apart—move feet and body in circle using right arm as a pivot; repeat using left arm.

Seal Walk

- Support body on hands and feet; keep feet together and legs straight; walk forward with hands; drag legs behind.

Wheelbarrow

- Walk on hands while partner holds and guides by holding ankles.

WINNER

Modified Push-Ups
Use basic starting position (p. 15) unless otherwise indicated.

Knee Push-Ups

Support weight on hands and knees—feet off floor.

Bend elbows and touch chin (nose, forehead, chest) to floor.

Return to original position and continue in this manner.

Wall Push-Ups

Stand with feet together 18 to 24 inches from a wall; extend arms from shoulders with hands flat against wall approximately shoulder width apart.

Bend elbows and touch chin (nose, forehead, chest) to wall.

Return to original position and continue in this manner.

STAR

Push-Ups

Use basic starting position (p. 15) unless otherwise indicated.

Bend elbows and touch chin (nose, forehead, chest) to floor.

Return to original position and continue in this manner.

One Leg Push-Ups

- Perform as *Push-Ups* (above) except raise and keep one leg extended throughout the exercise.

Chinese Push-Ups

- Make a window by allowing the thumbs and forefingers just to touch each other.
- Bend elbows and touch noise in the window.
- Return to original position and continue in this manner.

Tiger Push-Ups

- Stand with back to wall and heels one to two feet from the wall.
- Place feet on wall and walk backwards up wall until body is fully extended and supported on hands.
- Hold this position for five (10, 15, 20, 30) seconds,

or

- Bend elbows and touch chin (nose, forehead, chest) to floor; return to original position and continue in this manner.

CHAMP

Special Push-Ups

Use basic starting position (p. 15) unless otherwise indicated.

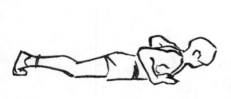

Pile Driver

Push vigorously into air and clap hands (hands and feet) together while in air.

Chest Slap

- Push vigorously into air and slap chest with both hands while in air.

17

In Orbit Push-Ups

Use basic starting position (p. 15) unless otherwise indicated.

Behind Back Push-Ups

- Push vigorously into air and clap hands together behind back while in air. (Do only on mats, grass, or other soft surfaces).

Superman Push-Ups

- Place right hand directly under chest and left hand on right — push up.

Extension Push-Ups

Extend arms fully above head and raise body from fingertips and toes.

ABDOMINAL ENDURANCE

Basic starting position for all activities at all levels unless otherwise indicated:

Extend legs with ankles about a foot apart.

Grasp hands behind neck with fingers interlaced.

Variations:

Use at all levels and with most activities.

- Extend arms fully overhead; fold arms across chest; place arms at sides.
- Hold legs and ankles down (partner or hooked under bar, chair, table, bench).
- Spread legs farther apart; bring legs closer together.

Helpful Hint:

- Increase or decrease the difficulty of activities by changing arm and leg positions in different combinations.

Warning:

Do not allow youngsters to bounce back off floor when doing a series of sit-ups.

See-Saw

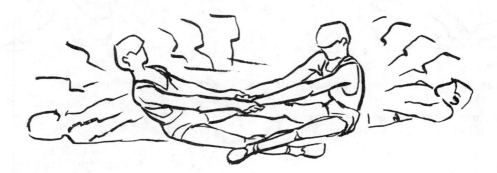

Sit with partner on floor and place legs inside (outside) of partner's legs; one partner lies on back; hold hands throughout activity.

Change positions so that partner on back is pulled to sitting position while other partner lies on back.

Continue in see-saw fashion.

Variations:

- Change speed of activity.
- Reduce amount of pulling assistance by top partner.
- Increase resistance provided by top partner by pushing instead of pulling.
- Come half way up and hold in this position for five (10, 15, 20, 30) seconds.

WINNER

Sit-Ups

Sit-up and turn trunk to right (left) touching left (right) elbow to right (left) thigh (knee).

Return to starting position.

Repeat using opposite elbow and thigh (knee).

Variations:

- Touch left elbow to left thigh (knee) and right elbow to right thigh (knee) simultaneously.
- Hold broom stick or wooden dowel behind back and under arm pits.

Bent-Leg Sit-Ups

Bend knees keeping feet flat on floor with (without) ankles held.

Sit-up and turn trunk to right (left) touching left (right) elbow to right (left) thigh (knee).

Return to starting position.

Repeat using opposite elbow and thigh (knee).

Variation:

- Touch left elbow to left thigh (knee) and right elbow to right thigh (knee) simultaneously.

CHAMP

Curl

Sit-up until waist (belt level) is just off floor.

Return to starting position.

Continue in slow rhythmic pattern.

Variation:

- Hold position for five (10, 15, 20, 30) seconds.

SUPER CHAMP

V-Up

Lift trunk and legs simultaneously to form a V.

Keep arms and legs straight, trying to touch toes with fingertips.

Return to starting position.

Continue in slow rhythmic pattern.

Variation:

- Hold V-position for five (10, 15, 20, 30) seconds.

BALANCE

ROOKIE

Basic Body Balances

Helpful Hints:

- Make designated movements without moving other parts of the body.
- Perform activities with eyes open and then closed.

Take position on hands, knees, and feet with legs and arms about shoulder width apart.

Move left (right) arm forward (backward, sideward) to shoulder level.

Extend left (right) leg backward.

Move arms and legs in various combinations —

- Lift both arms.
- Lift both feet.
- Lift arm and leg on same side of body.
- Lift arm and leg on opposite sides of body.
- Lift both arms and one (other) foot.
- Lift both feet and one (other) arm.
- Lift both feet and both arms (balance on knees).

Variations:

- Lift knees and support self on hands and toes; move arms and legs in various combinations —
  - ✓ Lift left (right) arm forward (backward, sideward) to shoulder level.
  - ✓ Extend left (right) leg backward.
  - ✓ Lift arm and leg on same side of body.
  - ✓ Lift arm and leg on opposite sides of body.
  - ✓ Kick both feet into air.
- Sit, raise buttocks off floor, and support body on hands and feet; move arms and legs in various combinations —
  - ✓ Extend left (right) leg forward.
  - ✓ Extend left (right) arm backward (forward, sideward).
  - ✓ Lift arm and leg on same side of body.
  - ✓ Lift arm and leg on opposite sides of body.
  - ✓ Kick both feet into air.
- Lie on side with arms, one on top of other, extended overhead and legs, one on top of other, fully extended; raise top arm and leg vertically attempting to make contact with hand and foot without bending elbow or knee; hold for designated count or length of time.

- Lie on back, bring legs to 45 degree angle, extend arms forward to touch toes, and hold balance on buttocks.

NOTE: Start youngster, if necessary, flat on his back or stomach rather than in support positions.

WINNER

Balance in Motion

Helpful Hints:

- Challenge youngsters by having them perform a variety of *Basic Body Balances* in motion such as animal walks, imitative activities, and in other original ways.
- Add variations by having youngsters move in different directions (foward, backward, sideward, over and under obstacles), in different ways (lift, carry, or extend arms and legs in various combinations), and at different speeds (slow, slower, fast, faster).
- Perform activities with eyes open and then closed.

Beetle

Creep on hands and knees.

Monster

Support body on hands and feet; walk, keeping arms and legs straight.

Bear Walk

Support body on hands and feet; walk by moving right arm and right leg together, then left arm and left leg; keep arms and legs straight.

Lame Dog

Support body on hands and feet, elevate left (right) leg, and move on both hands and right (left) foot; change position of feet after going a designated distance.

Crab

Sit, raise buttocks off floor, support body on hands and feet, and move backward (sideward).

Spider

Sit, raise buttocks off floor, support body on hands and feet, and move forward (sideward).

Seal

Support body on hands and feet; keep feet together and legs straight; walk forward with hands; drag legs behind.

Coffee Grinder

Support body on right arm and both feet; keep arm and legs fully extended with feet slightly apart; move feet and body in circle using right arm as a pivot; repeat using left arm.

Leaning Tower

Support body on extended right arm and hand and side of right foot; hold left arm against side and place left leg on top of right leg; extend left arm straight up and hold position for five (10, 15, 20) seconds; return to starting position, extend left leg straight up and hold for designated time; return to starting position, extend both left arm and leg and hold for designated time. Rest between different movements if necessary and repeat movements with right arm and leg.

Crazy Knees

Balance and walk on knees.

STAR

Stork Stand Progression

Helpful Hints:

- Make designated movements without moving other parts of the body.
- Hold each position for five (10, 15, 20, 30) seconds.
- Peform activities with eyes open and then closed.

Stand on left foot with hands on hips and right foot placed against inside of left knee; reverse and stand on right foot with left foot placed against inside of right knee.

Variations:

- Fold arms across chest.
- Hold hands against thighs.
- Extend arms above head.
- Extend arms to sides at shoulder level.
- Extend arms in front of body at shoulder level.
- Hold one arm in one position and other arm in another position (such as high-low; front-back; up-down; front-side).
- Hold free foot close to ground (forward, backward, sideward, different heights).
- Bend forward at waist until upper body is parallel to floor; extend free leg directly back until foot is held about shoulder level; keep extended leg straight, head up, and arms directly to sides at shoulder level.
- Perform other tasks while holding balance—
  ✓ Bounce a ball.
  ✓ Play catch.
  ✓ Hold objects (beanbags, weighted bleach bottles) of different weights in each hand.
  ✓ Balance objects (beanbags, balls) on different parts of body (palm of hand, back of hand, arm, elbow, head, shoulder).

And Away We Go

Helpful Hints:

- Use lines on floor, designated rows of floor tiles, tempra, contact paper, chalk, or masking tape lines, or items such as clothesline stretched on floors as boundaries.
- Make boundaries increasingly narrow until youngsters are performing activities on line or object.
- Make boundaries in different shapes (circles, triangles, squares, rectangles, diamonds, snail, maze).
- Add variations by having youngsters move in different directions (foward, backward, sideward), over and under obstacles, in different ways (lift, carry, or extend arms in various directions) and at different speeds (slow, slower, fast, faster).
- Add additional variations by having youngsters move on different parts of foot (toes, heels, outside, inside), perform other tasks (bounce a ball, play catch, hold objects of different weights in each hand, balance objects on different parts of body, jump rope, turn a hoop, wheelbarrow), and use different locomotor movements (walk, jump, hop, slide, leap, gallop).

Balance Board Activities

Helpful Hints:

- Make balance boards 16" x 16" x ½" with two 2" x 4" bases 16" (8", 4", 2", 1") per board.
- Introduce activities with balance board flat on floor and then place two 16" x 2" x 4" bases under balance board so that height off floor is increased gradually; criss cross other 2" x 4" bases under main balance board to increase height even more.
- Reduce support under balance board by using smaller 2" x 4" bases.
- Use only one 16" base the width of the balance board; turn length of balance board; reduce support by using smaller 2" x 4" bases; secure supports 4" and smaller with a wing nut or wooden peg.
- Use other objects such as tires and inner tubes.
- Devise other types of balance boards that offer additional challenges for youngsters—curve bottom support, make balance board itself smaller, attach top of board to springs.
- Perform *Basic Body Balances* (p. 21) and *Stork Stand Progression* (p. 22).

Activities

- Perform *Basic Body Balances* (p. 21) and *Stork Stand Progressions* (p. 22).
- Perform see-saw activities when balance board is supported on one 2" x 4" base.

- Use tiles, wooden blocks, contact paper cut in various shapes, cinder block, bricks, or other objects for youngsters to move across while performing various activities.
- Perform activities with eyes open and then closed.

Activities

- Perform *Basic Body Balances* (p. 21), *Balance in Motion Activities*, (p. 21), and *Stork Stand Progression* (p. 22) within increasingly narrow boundaries.
- Walk (heel-toe, touch knee to heel) between designated points—increase distances and reduce width of boundaries gradually.
- Perform jump turns of increasing amounts (quarter, half, three-quarter, full, one and a quarter) within increasingly narrow boundaries.
- Perform various combinations such as walk from one point to another in one manner and return in another (walk to a point, turn, continue in another way).
- Devise own activities, combinations, and routines.

SUPER CHAMP

- Work with a partner in different activities on balance boards of various sizes and shapes.
- Devise own activities, combinations, and routines.

Balance Beam Activities

Helpful Hints:

- Use regulation low or high balance beam.
- Devise own balance beam from 2" x 4" boards; construct so either 4" or 2" side can be used.
- Introduce graduated balance beams in which sections get increasingly narrow (6", 4", 2", 1"); place in different patterns (straight, W, V, N, M, L).
- Perform activities with eyes open and then closed.

Activities

- Perform *Basic Body Balances* (p. 21), *Balance in Motion Activities* (p. 21), *Stork Stand Progression* (p. 22) and *And Away We Go Progression* (p. 23) on increasingly narrow balance beams.
- Perform various combative (hand wrestling, chicken fighting, bulling) activities with a partner.
- Devise own activities, combinations, and routines.

POWER/SPEED

ROOKIE

Vertical Jumps

Stand near a wall.

Swing arms and reach as high as possible while jumping.

Variations:

- Mark wall with chalk at peak of jump—record best jump and try to make a higher mark each practice session.
- Touch (grasp) a broom stick (wooden dowel, ruler, yard stick, toy, stuffed animal) held at increasing heights near wall by partner or coach.
- Make an all out jump and mark height in some way; jump five (10, 15, 20) times or for five (10, 15, 20) seconds and try to better first jump on as many of following jumps as possible.
- Move away from wall and jump as high as possible.
- Jump on inner-tubes (bounce boards, tire casings, trampolets, or other bouncy objects) to help get feel and idea of lifting the body into the air.

WINNER

Piston

Sit on floor with back straight, legs extended, feet together, and back of thighs flat on floor.

Grasp hands behind neck with fingers interlocked and elbows as far back as possible.

Lift one heel about six inches off floor and bring knee as far back toward chest as possible.

Return to starting position by straightening leg.

Continue for designated repetitions or length of time.

Repeat using other leg.

Variations:

- Place hands on floor near buttocks.
- Place hands on hips.
- Fold hands across chest.

- Touch heel to floor on each extension.
- Alternate legs.
- Use both legs simultaneously.

STAR

Partner Push

NOTE: B indicates *bottom* partner.
T indicates *top* partner.

(B) Lie on back with hands flat on floor near thighs and legs extended upward at a 45 degree angle.

(T) Place chest on soles of partner's feet; extend legs back so body is straight; grasp partner's legs and/or keep your legs a shoulder width apart for balance and control if necessary.

(T) Force partner's legs to his chest.

(B) Resist partner's movement and let legs bend slowly until knees touch chest (most youngsters can resist strongly enough to prevent any movement of their legs; work to obtain appropriate amount of resistance).

(B) Extend legs and push partner back to starting position.

(T) Provide appropriate amount of resistance.

Reverse positions after designated length of time or number of repetitions.

Variation:

- Use one leg for designated period and then the other; (T) legs in same position as above or outside leg near buttocks of partner and inside leg extended straight back and behind body.

> *The test of our progress is not whether we add more to the abundance of those who have much; it is whether we provide enough for those who have too little.*
>
> *Franklin D. Roosevelt*

CHAMP

Inverted Bicycle

Lie on back with legs and hips raised to vertical position with elbows on floor; support hips with hands.

Move legs vigorously as if pedaling a bicycle.

Variation:

- Lean back on elbows and pedal with legs extended about 45 degrees.

SUPER CHAMP

Mountain Climber

Squat with hands on floor; point fingers forward and extend one leg fully to rear.

Reverse position of feet by bringing rear foot to hands and extending front foot backward in one motion.

Continue in rhythmic pattern.

Variation:

- Work both legs simultaneously rather than alternately.

> *If you would cultivate the intelligence of your pupil, give his body continued exercise, make him robust and sound in order to make him wise and reasonable.*
>
> *Rosseau*

AGILITY

ROOKIE

Side Step

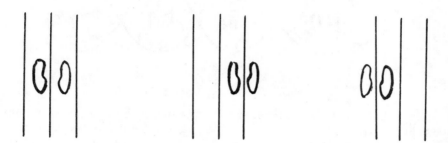

Mark three lines as shown; substitute ropes for marked lines.

Start with both feet on center line.

Move left foot over left line.

Variations:
- Use two lines instead of three.
- Move both feet over outside line when stepping in either direction.
- Jump so both feet go over outside line when moving in either direction.
- Place right foot on (over) left line and return to center line; place left foot on (over) right line and return to center line; continue this pattern.
- Jump and make a quarter (half, three-quarter) turn landing on (beyond) an outside line; return to starting position by jumping and turning in opposite direction.
- Do continuous series of quarter (half, full) turns in clockwise (counterclockwise) direc-

Return to center line.

Move right foot over right line.

Return to center line.

Continue in this manner.

tion landing on (beyond) each outside line and/or on center line each time.
- Move feet so they land between lines; return to starting position and continue this pattern.
- Hop alternately landing with left foot between center and left lines and right foot between center and right lines; hop rhythmically taking two hops left and then two right or four left and two right; develop own patterns.
- Start outside of right line; hop landing between right and center lines on left foot; change feet landing on right foot; hop landing between center and left lines on left foot; change feet landing on right foot; hop landing outside left line on left foot; return to starting position moving to right and leading with right foot.

WINNER

Shuttle Run

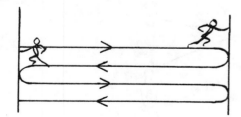

Mark two lines as shown; substitute bicycle tires (automobile tires, hoops, ropes, or similar objects) for marked lines.

Start behind one line and run back and forth between lines for designated number of laps or period of time.

Variations:
- Increase the number of laps or time of run.
- Increase distance between lines.
- Touch lines with specific parts of body such as feet, hands, knees, elbows, head.
- Place specific parts of body in objects in various combinations (e.g., right hand and left foot; left elbow, left knee, and head).
- Transfer objects from one line (object) to the other.
- Walk, jump, hop, gallop, skip, or imitate animals such as crab, spider, seal, bear, lame dog.

Dodging Run

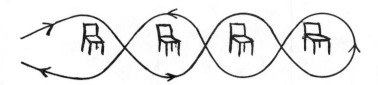

Variations:

- Increase or decrease number of objects and/ or distance between them.
- Go completely clockwise (counterclockwise) around each object before moving to the next one.
- Alternate directions around objects—go completely clockwise around the first, counterclockwise around the second, and so on.
- Walk, jump, hop, gallop, skip, or imitate animals such as crab, spider, seal, bear, lame dog.

Set up chairs (bleach bottles, milk cartons, bowling pins, tires) as shown.

Start at base line and run to left of first object, to right of second object, to left of third object, around the fourth object, to right of third, to left of second, to right of first, and back to base line.

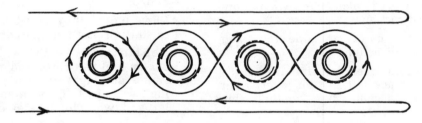

Start on stomach (back) at starting line; rise on signal, run to second line, return to first object, follow basic in-and-out pattern up and back, and then run to second line and back to starting line.

CHAMP

Zig Zag Run

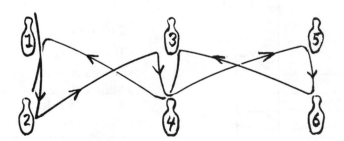

Place six tires (chairs, bowling pins, milk cartons, bleach bottles, marks on floor) in two lines as shown.

Number each object with one, three, and five on left and two, four, and six on right; use

contact paper arrows of different colors to show pattern if necessary.

Start at one, run to two and touch it, run to three and touch it, continue in order to four, five, six, three, four, one, two.

Variations:

- Increase number of objects and/or distance between them.
- Touch objects with specific parts of body such as feet, hands, knees, elbows, head; touch all objects with same (different) parts of body.

- Run completely around each object.
- Walk, jump, hop, gallop, skip, or imitate animals such as crab, spider, seal, bear, lame dog.

SUPER CHAMP

Boomerang

Place three chairs (tires, bowling pins, milk cartons, bleach bottles, marks on floor) as shown.

Number objects one, two, and three as shown; place contact paper arrows on floor if necessary to show pattern.

Start at baseline and run clockwise around each chair in succession, one, then two, and three, and finally back to baseline.

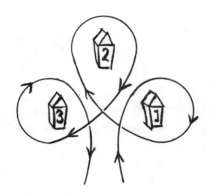

Variations:

- Make a figure-eight pattern around two chairs.
- Add a fourth chair and run clockwise pattern.
- Make alternate figure-eight patterns around north-south (two-four) and east-west (one-three) chairs (four chairs in all).

- Develop own patterns and movements around chairs.
- Increase number of trips or time patterns.
- Walk, jump, hop, gallop, skip, or imitate animals such as crab, spider, seal, bear, lame dog.

COORDINATION

ROOKIE

Jump and Turn

Draw a circle on the floor approximately 18 inches in diameter with at least eight equally spaced lines coming from center of circle.

Stand in middle of circle with feet pointing to one line.

Jump and turn as far as possible and land with both feet together on another line.

Continue to jump in this manner in the same (opposite) direction.

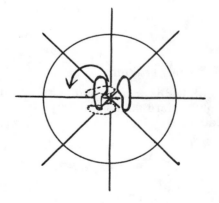

Variations:

- Jump to assigned lines or a designated distance such as quarter (half, three-quarter, full, one-and-a quarter) turn, or until facing a designated object such as a clock (window, chalkboard, basket, office, door).

- Use bicycle tires, automobile tires, hoops, ropes, contact paper targets, or similar objects of different sizes as a substitute for circle.

Jumping Jack

Start at attention.

Swing arms sideward and upward; touch palms above head keeping arms straight.

Move feet sideward and apart as arms are moved.

Return to starting position and repeat as often as desired.

Variations:

- Move feet only.
- Bring arms only to shoulder level.
- Raise arms straight forward.
- Touch fingers to shoulders.
- Combine different arm and foot movements.
- Go through basic movements lying on floor.

STAR

Sensational Seven

One

Starting Positions

Stand with hands at sides and feet slightly more than shoulder width apart.

Movements

(a) Move feet together and swing arms overhead and clap.

(b) Return to starting position and repeat as often as desired.

Two

Stand at attention.

(a) Move (jump) feet apart and swing arms to side at shoulder level.

(b) Move (jump) feet together and swing arms to front at shoulder level.

(c) Move (jump) to (a) position.

(d) Return to attention and repeat as often as desired.

Three

Stand at attention.

(a) Move (jump) feet apart and swing arms to front at shoulder level.

(b) Move (jump) feet together and swing arms to sides at shoulder level.

(c) Move (jump) to (a) position.

(d) Return to attention and repeat as often as desired.

Four

Stand at attention.

(a) Move (jump) right foot in front; left foot lands in starting position and swing arms to front at shoulder level.

(b) Move (jump) right foot to side; left foot lands in starting position and swing arms to side at shoulder level.

(c) Move (jump) to (a) position.

(d) Return to attention.

(e) Continue with left foot and repeat as often as desired.

Five

Stand at attention.

(a) Move (jump) right foot in front; left foot lands in starting position and swing arms to side at shoulder level.

(b) Move (jump) right foot to side; left foot lands in starting position and swing arms to front at shoulder level.

(c) Move (jump) to (a) position.

(d) Return to attention.

(e) Continue with left foot and repeat as often as desired.

Six

Stand with feet apart and arms to side at shoulder level.

(a) Move (jump) right foot to front, left foot to rear and behind right; swing arms to front at shoulder level.

(b) Move (jump) feet apart and swing arms back to side at shoulder level.

(c) Move (jump) left foot to front, right foot to rear and behind left, and swing arms up over head and clap.

(d) Move (jump) feet apart and bring arms to side at shoulder level (starting position).

(e) Repeat as often as desired.

Seven

Stand with feet apart and arms to front at shoulder level.

(a) Move (jump) right foot to front, left foot to rear and behind right; swing arms to side at shoulder level.

(b) Move (jump) feet apart and swing arms up over head and clap.

(c) Move (jump) left foot to front, right foot to rear and behind left; swing arms to side at shoulder level.

(d) Move (jump) feet apart and swing arms to front at shoulder level (starting position).

(e) Repeat as often as desired.

SENSATIONAL!!!!

Variation:

• Devise your own combinations with different arm and foot movements.

31

CHAMP

Squat Thrust Series

Start at attention.

Bend knees and place hands on floor in front of feet with arms between (outside of, in front of) legs.

Thrust legs back so body is straight from shoulders to feet (push-up position).

Return to squat position and then to attention.

Repeat as often as desired.

Variations:

- Add a push-up to the sequence.
- Increase one push-up (two counts) with each repetition.
- Include any of the more difficult push-ups (pp. 16-18).
- Use one arm only.
- Touch fingertips to toes and keep knees straight; squat and extend arms forward at shoulder level; place hands on floor and thrust legs back and forth returning to squat position with arms extended from shoulders; touch fingertips to toes and return to standing position and then to attention.

SUPER CHAMP

Astronaut Drills

Helpful Hints:

- Conduct drills quickly and in rapid succession.
- Have youngsters move from position to position on signal.
- Vary order in which directions are given to keep youngsters alert.
- Add new positions to those listed.

Go!

Run in place keeping knees high and pumping arms vigorously.

Front!

Move to prone position keeping palms of hands flat on floor directly under shoulders and legs together and straight.

Back!

Lie flat on back with arms extended along side of body, palms down, and legs together and straight.

Side!

Lie on either side (indicate right or left side if youngsters identify right from left).

Leg-Up!

Lie on side and lift top leg straight up from hip; hold this position until next direction is given.

Push-Up!

Do push-ups until next direction is given.

Sit-Up!

Do sit-ups until next direction is given.

Putting It Together:

Go! - Back! - Front! - Go! - Side! - Leg-Up! - Left Side! - Back! - Go! Push-Up! - Back! - Sit-Up! - Go!

CARDIORESPIRATORY ENDURANCE

ROOKIE

Bench Step

Helpful Hint:

- Use music, including records to sound a cadence; drums, cymbals, clapping, or words are also effective for this purpose.

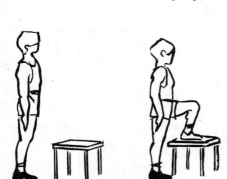

Use benches (chairs, stools) that are at least 15-inches high.

Face bench and alternately step up and down to a rhythm of left up, right up, left down, right down.

Repeat for 30 seconds (one to five minutes) at 30 (20, 40) steps per minute; increase time and/or speed as youngsters get in better condition.

WINNER

The Runner

Run in place landing low on balls of feet.

Lift knees to waist or higher and pump arms vigorously.

Variations:

- Lift feet only about an inch off floor.
- Run for a designated number of steps or specific length of time (20, 30, 60 seconds); rest for a specific length of time and then run again; increase length of run and number of running periods and decrease length of rest periods.

- Run up short steep hills (walk or jog down).
- Run up flights of steps (walk down).
- Hold arms so hands are at thigh (waist, abdomen, chest) level and touch knees to hands.
- Do as *Tortoise and Hare* running very slowly and then very rapidly.

STAR

Crazy Legs

(Run in Place — Windshield Wiper — Pogo Spring)

Helpful Hints:

- Perform each of three activities for a designated length of time or a stipulated number of steps.
- Add variations to challenge youngsters and to maintain interest.

Run in Place

Run in place landing low on balls of feet.

Variations:

- Bounce on both feet.
- Lift knees high.
- Lift feet only about an inch off floor.

Windshield Wiper

Move legs alternately astride and together.

Variations:

- Crisscross legs.
- Move legs alternately astride and crisscross.

Pogo Spring

Move legs alternately forward and back.

Variation:

- Move legs alternately forward/back and astride/together.

Variations:

- Change movement on signal (i.e., Run — Pogo Spring — Windshield Wiper; Pogo Spring — Run — Windshield Wiper; Windshield Wiper — Pogo Spring — Run).

- Perform each activity in sequence for a designated number of counts (four, eight, sixteen); continue for a designated length of time or a stipulated number of total counts.

CHAMP

Run/Walk

- Run and walk predetermined distances.
- Increase length, time, and speed of running gradually and decrease amount of walking.
- Set up tracks or courses in gymnasium, on blacktop area, tennis court, playfield, around baseball or softball diamond, or between two points; use chairs (tires, bleach bottles, milk cartons, bowling pins, traffic cones, marked lines) to set off track or course.
- Use patterns such as —

  √ Run short sides and walk long sides.

  √ Run long sides and walk short sides.

  √ Run a short and long side and walk a short and long side.

  √ Run a short and long side and walk a short side; run a long and short side and walk a long side; continue to run two sides and walk one side.

  √ Run three sides—short, long, short—and walk one long side.

  √ Run three sides—long, short, long—and walk one short side.

  √ Run four sides (one lap) and walk two sides (half-lap).

  √ Run two laps and walk one lap.

  √ Run four laps and walk half-lap.

  √ Increase running and decrease walking as condition and ability of youngsters improve.

Helpful Hints:

- Devise a variety of ways to make this activity more enjoyable—chase the youngster; have him chase you; run with him; introduce games.
- Time youngsters for various distances and laps to encourage them to run faster and longer.

Roadwork

Helpful Hints:

- Set up jogging-running courses on park greens, stadium turf, golf courses, wooded areas, and similar places.
- Use natural surroundings — fallen tree branches and trunks, fences, small ditches, culverts, hills, logs, large rocks, and other obstacles found in the local environment.
- Adapt less natural outdoor surroundings such as playgrounds, stadiums, school yards, large open areas, residential facility campuses, home yards, as well as indoor areas such as gymnasiums, halls, multi-purpose rooms, auditoriums, and cafetoriums for roadwork.
- Include a variety of activities in each roadwork session — locomotor activities such as walking, jogging, shuffling, running, sprinting; formal exercises, stunts and self-testing activities, partner activities, combatives; incorporate other locomotor activities such as jumping, hopping, skipping, galloping, leaping, and sliding.
- Develop patterns, distance, and length of time for roadwork sessions according to age, ability, and condition of youngsters — an entire practice session or a conditioning/fitness session can be developed around roadwork.
- Play follow the leader, changing leaders often and having last youngster run to front to become leader.
- Adjust speed of run to slowest individual in group and time and length of session to individual with least stamina.

Sample Roadwork Session

(35 to 45 minutes — adapt and shorten according to each individual situation)

- Run in place until entire group has assembled.
- Jog 50 to 200 yards while swinging arms in various ways.
- Jump to head an imaginary soccer ball or to touch the leaf of branches of a tree — see who can jump the highest.
- Swim an imaginary river, pond, lake, or pool.
- Balance in a variety of ways.
- Jog 75 to 150 yards and change to race walking for an additional 50 to 100 yards.
- Do simple individual tumbling stunts such as forward, backward, and side rolls.
- Carry a partner piggy-back; change after 25 to 30 yards.
- Shadow box several rounds with an imaginary opponent.
- Run between two points with a partner.
- Jog at a faster pace for 50 to 200 yards.
- Jump over various obstacles or barriers; hop over others.
- Sprint 50 yards with a partner.
- Walk or amble 100 yards.
- Do push-ups, sit-ups, partner pull-ups, piston, partner-push, and other exercises.
- Jog 100 to 200 yards zig zag fashion.
- Play follow the leader.
- Jump and vault over various objects.
- Walk at a fast pace for 100 yards.
- Get a partner for combative activities such as hand wrestling, hand-tug-o-war, chicken fight.
- Do a variety of individual stunts such as cartwheel, walk on hands, handsprings.
- Run at easy, steady pace for 100 to 200 yards.
- Get a partner for various partner stunts such as centipede, wheelbarrow, fireman's carry.
- Sprint back to start gradually increasing distance of sprint from 100 to 400 yards.

---

*If a man does not keep pace
With his companions, perhaps it is because
he hears a different drummer.
Let him step to the music which he hears,
however measured or far away.*

Henry David Thoreau

TEAM LOG ACTIVITIES

Team log activities get youngsters used to working together, cooperating, and learning the importance of teamwork through a form of resistance exercises.

Helpful Hints:

- Obtain logs 12 to 14 feet long, six to eight inches in diameter, which weigh between 100 and 300 pounds, depending upon size, strength, and ability of youngsters.
- Sand logs, fill all cracks with putty or plastic wood, and coat with shellac, floor sealer, or other type of durable finish.
- Mark each log so youngsters know where to stand and where to grip the log.

- Let five or six youngsters about the same height work as a unit; all youngsters on same side of log unless otherwise indicated.
- Provide a variety of lifting signals for youngsters; use verbal commands, whistle, visual signals, drum beat; encourage groups to develop their own ways of coordinating movements.
- Increase cadence and speed of movements as youngsters gain experience and confidence in handling logs.
- Devise your own bending, lifting, tossing activities involving combinations of movements and positions (sitting, standing, kneeling). Adapt activities for relays, games, and in other fun ways.

Starting Positions

Right (left) shoulder

Balance log on shoulder with both hands; spread feet slightly more than a shoulder width apart.

Waist

Hold log waist high with arms straight and fingers laced underneath log; bend body slightly back with chest lifted and arched; keep feet slightly more than a shoulder width apart.

Chest

Hold log high on chest with both arms under and around the log; keep upper arms parallel to ground and feet slightly more than a shoulder width apart.

Activities	Starting Positions	Movements
Straddle Jump	Hold log in any starting position.	Jump feet together and apart in various cadences.
Log Rolling	Take position on one side of log according to way in which it is to be rolled.	Roll log with one hand (two hands, one foot, two feet, head).
Push-Up	Lie on floor; hold log in chest position.	Lift log straight up from chest; return to chest position.
Sit-Up	Lie on floor; hold log in chest position.	Move to sitting position; return to lying position.

Forward Bender	Hold log in chest position with knees slightly bent.	Bend forward from waist; return to upright position.
Overhead Lift	Start from right shoulder position; try from kneeling or sitting position, as well as standing.	Lift log overhead and down to left shoulder; lift from left shoulder returning log to right shoulder.
Overhead Toss	Start from right (left) shoulder position; bend the knees to a quarter-squat position.	Straighten knees and toss log into air; catch log with both hands and lower it toward opposite shoulder; lower body to quarter-squat position as log is caught; continue tossing, catching, and changing shoulders.
Team Toss	Have two teams stand facing each other about three to six paces apart; start log in waist position and move it to bend of both arms holding with an underhand grip.	Toss log to other team which catches it and tosses it back; continue tossing log back and forth.
Log Push	Have two teams lie down on floor with log between them; have each youngster place his hands on log and push as hard as possible.	Force other team back across line or goal.
Pivot Circle	Hold log in chest position; try other starting positions for variation.	Move in circle with one of end men serving as the center or pivot point; move forward (backward) in various ways (walk, run, jump, hop, skip, gallop).
Wagon Wheel	Have three youngsters on one side of log and three youngsters on other side of log with all facing the log.	Walk around in a circle; vary speed; change to fast walk (run, jump, hop, skip, gallop).
Obstacle Course	Have four youngsters hold log, two at each end; place logs at regular intervals.	Adjust height of each log so youngsters hurdle, vault or jump over them, crawl under or climb over them, or perform a combination of activities.

Sit-Up

Wagon Wheel

Log Push

RESISTANCE ACTIVITIES
(Weight Training)

Resistance activities are to develop strength and endurance by making muscles work harder and longer. Weight training or lifting is the most common type of resistance activity; barbells, bars, and weights are not needed for these activities! Effective and inexpensive substitutes include:

- Broomsticks or wooden dowels with objects such as doorknobs attached.
- Car axles.
- Folding chairs.
- Window sash weights.
- Homemade barbells constructed with broomsticks or wooden dowels and different size tin cans filled with various amounts of cement.
- Bleach bottles filled with sand—increase amount of sand as youngsters get stronger.
- Stuffed animals—increase weight by putting more buckshot or sand in stuffed tiger, cat, or dog.
- Logs—use regular fireplace logs or make special exercise logs about 10-12 inches long, five to ten inches in diameter, and about one-tenth of the youngster's weight.

Helpful Hints:

- Concentrate on arms, shoulders, and chest since legs are best developed by running.
- Perform a given activity *between eight and twelve times*. More than 12 times indicates too little weight and it should be increased; less than eight times indicates too much weight and it should be decreased.
- Perform all activities in a *slow, smooth,* and *controlled* manner.
- Complete all movements and go through a full range of motion in all activities.
- Emphasize proper breath control by *inhaling* when lifting and *exhaling* while returning weight to starting position.
- Place feet a natural standing width apart and space hands evenly on bar unless otherwise indicated.

Activities	Starting Positions	Movements
Press	Start weight from chest.	Lift weight over head in one continuous movement; extend arms fully until elbows are straight; lower weight to chest.
Behind Neck Press	Start weight from chest.	Lift weight over head and lower to a position behind neck; lift and lower weight from behind neck.
Bench Press	Lie on floor or bench; start weight from chest.	Perform same movements as in *press.*
Military Press	Sit on chair, bench, or floor; start weight from chest.	Perform same movements as in *press* or *behind neck press.*
Curl	Start weight at thigh level with palms of hands facing away from body.	Bend elbows and lift weight to shoulder level without bending or rocking body; lower weight to starting position.
Reverse Curl	Start weight at thigh level with palms facing toward body.	Perform same movements as in *curl.*
Rowing	Place feet slightly more than shoulder width apart; bend forward from waist until upper body is parallel to floor; hold weight off floor at ankle level.	Lift weight until it touches chest; lower weight to starting position.
Upright Rowing	Hold weight at shoulder level with hands as close together as possible; keep elbows higher than bar at all times.	Lower weight until elbows are straight; lift weight to starting position.
Pull Over	Lie on floor or bench with arms extended over head; keep arms straight at all times.	Lift weight until it is directly over chest; lower weight until it rests on thighs; lift weight to position over chest and then to starting position.
Bent Arm Pull Over	Lie on floor or bench; keep elbows bent fully throughout movements.	Bring weight as far forward as possible; return to starting position.

Variations:

- Perform all activities with individual resistance objects held in one or both hands.
- Introduce a variety of swinging activities with individual resistance objects held in one or both hands:
- Swing weight freely.
- Swing weight between legs.
- Pick up weight, swing it high above head (in front or to side of body), bring it down, and place at side of one foot.
- Swing weight from side to side turning body as far as possible.
- Twist and turn weight over head.

CHAIR ACTIVITIES

Chairs are adaptable to a variety of fitness activities that interest youngsters of different ages and at various functional levels. *Any kind of chair a child can handle easily becomes a fitness chair.* Chair activities can be done in classrooms, at home, or in other small spaces; they provide ready-made rainy-day activity. Place chairs in rows so activities can be individual or group in nature or done as a routine.

- *Stand up/sit down*—stand up and sit down on command or signal; perform at various speeds.
- *Around the chair*—walk, jog, skip, hop, gallop, slide, leap, or run around own chair.
- *Around the row*—run, leap, slide, gallop, hop, skip, jog, or walk around chairs in own row; use various animal walks and imitative activities.
- *Around all the rows*—move to the front of own row; youngsters in right-most row start to run around all rows, circling to the right. As the last person in each row begins to run, youngsters in the next row fall in behind him and start to run; run in place while waiting to run. Add variety by having the group run the first lap, skip the second, gallop the third, and walk the fourth.

- *Circle activities*—perform various activities listed with chairs in circle rather than rows; place a mat in the middle of the circle and have individuals perform stunts or other activities when they are called; play follow the leader with each youngster getting a chance to be leader; introduce add-on so that each participant does a new stunt in addition to the ones performed by those who went before him; play various circle games.
- *Chair step*—step on and off chairs to commands up right, up left, down right, down left; vary the tempo.
- *Chair jump*—stand on chair, jump off and land on both feet; follow with a stunt or activity of another kind.
- *Lift the chair*—lift the chair on command and perform various resistance activities (see p. 38 for specific activities and additional suggestions).
- *Chair obstacles*—use chairs as obstacles for youngsters to move around, go over and under, perform activities on and with, and to devise their own confidence courses.

Frequently it is attention rather than skilled guidance that these children need, and neglect often results from the belief of the staff that they lack the expertise to accomplish meaningful results.

Dr. Edward J. Waterhouse
New Zealand

CONFIDENCE COURSES

Confidence courses promote fitness through continuous movement in overcoming a series of obstacles requiring use of one or more components of fitness. Obstacles provide increasing challenges for youngsters and promote confidence in their ability and in themselves as each successive hurdle is cleared.

Confidence courses can include ropes, culverts, horizontal/parallel/turning/stall bars, horizontal ladders, beams/boards/rails, walls, fences, jungle gyms, tires, ramps, and anything else to challenge and excite youngsters as they climb, swing, hang, crawl, creep, balance, push, pull, and jump. Plan confidence courses with obstacles of various sizes—one scaling wall will challenge some youngsters, be too low for others, and look like a mountain to still others. Two or three scaling walls of different heights provide for the timid, unskilled, and awkward and at the same time challenge the bold, skilled, and agile. These courses can be used for overall conditioning, to overcome weak areas, and for work in specific Special Olympics events.

Devices incorporated into obstacle courses can be flexible and used in many ways:

- Have youngsters run over confidence course one, two, or three times, or go as far as they can in a specified time: regulate intensity of workout by controlling number of times course is covered or repetitions at each obstacle or station, or by total amount of time allocated.

- Use each obstacle as an activity or exercise station to emphasize specific component of fitness. Post printed cards at each station to tell exactly what is to be done. For nonreaders, use drawings, stick figures, or pictures to illustrate activities; use squad leaders, older youngsters, or aides to assist at different stations.

SELECTED CONDITIONING/FITNESS REFERENCES

American Association for Health, Physical Education, and Recreation. *Special Fitness Test Manual for the Mentally Retarded.* Washington, D.C.: The Association (1201 16th St., N.W.), 1968.

Department of the Army. *Physical Conditioning (TM 21-200).* Washington, D.C.: Department of the Army, 1957.

Hayden, Frank J. *Physical Fitness for the Mentally Retarded.* Ontario, Canada: Metropolitan Toronto Association for Retarded Children, 1964.

Hillcourt, William. *Your Guide to Fitness.* New York, New York: Western Publishing Co., Golden Press Division, 1968. (Distributed by the Quaker Oats Company, Chicago, Illinois.)

President's Council on Physical Fitness. *Adult Physical Fitness: A Program for Men and Women.* Washington, D.C.: Superintendent of Documents, U.S. Government Printing Office, 1963.

President's Council on Youth Fitness. *Youth Physical Fitness: Suggested Elements of a School-Centered Program (Parts One and Two).* Washington, D.C.: Superintendent of Documents, U.S. Government Printing Office, 1961.

Royal Canadian Air Force. *Royal Canadian Air Force Exercise Plans for Physical Fitness.* Mt. Vernon, New York: This Week Magazine.

Sandard Brands, Incorporated. *Mr. Peanut's Guide to Physical Fitness.* New York, New York: Standard Brands Educational Service (P.O. Box 2695, Grand Central Station), 1967.

Track and Field

Youngsters must be in good physical condition to be successful in track and field. Someone must stimulate them to train, run, compete, and strive continuously to develop fitness for track and field. Start each practice session with appropriate conditioning and warm-up activities as described in the conditioning and fitness section (pp. 6-40). Since flexibility and loose muscle action are vital to success in all Special Olympics track and field events, bending, stretching, and flexibility exercises must be stressed. A special series, *Flexible Five*, (p. 64), designed to develop flexibility of thighs and calves, must be a part of every practice session and premeet warm-up to prevent sore muscles and injuries and to promote best performances.

Ten practice cycles have been developed to help coaches organize and plan practice sessions. In addition, fundamentals, teaching progressions, drills, exercises, fun activities, and helpful hints are provided for each event. Cycles and information about each event can be adapted regardless of abilities of youngsters, available facilities, and time for practice. Cycles are based on the following assumptions:

- Practice sessions are held five days a week with Friday set aside for competition.
- Each practice session lasts 60 minutes with 75 minutes preferred.

Cycle 1 is largely exploratory in nature and designed to help determine each youngster's background, experience, and ability in fundamental skills needed for success in Special Olympics track and field events. Cycles 2–7 provide opportunities for youngsters to learn and practice all events. Cycles 8–10 are designed to prepare youngsters to compete in specific events.

It is imperative that milers be identified early so they can begin the arduous training as soon as possible—*they must have at least ten weeks practice before actual Special Olympics competition.* In addition to the 10 week practice period, all youngsters interested in running the mile should be encouraged to workout four to six weeks before formal practice begins. Refer to conditioning and fitness section (pp. 6 - 40) for specific suggestions.

The 300 yard run is considered the key running event for all participants other than milers. All 50 yard sprinters and relay men can benefit by training for the 300 since it is basically an endurance sprint involving all skills needed in the shorter distances. Participants in other events must run to condition their legs for jumping and throwing. They must have variety in their workouts since too much jumping or throwing causes leg or arm fatigue, reduces competitive efficiency, and makes injuries more likely—use 300 yard practice patterns to provide balanced preparation for high jump, standing long jump, and softball throw.

Teach everyone the fundamentals of relay running since preparing for this event is fun and gives youngsters the kind of responsibility that comes with being on a team and working closely with other youngsters.

Develop team spirit by impressing each youngster with the fact that he is not alone when competing in the 50 yard dash, the 300 yard run, the mile, or facing a bar inches over his head. The whole team is rooting for him, pulling for him, and encouraging him to run faster, jump higher, throw further, and to win, but most of all to do his best. And each in turn, as a loyal teammate, must encourage others to try harder, play harder, and do well.

Out of Special Olympics comradeship and mutual experiences come friendships that may last a lifetime and which transcend the immediate benefits of athletics and sports as important as they are.

Success in track and field requires willingness to work, get in condition, stay in shape, and master fundamentals of specific events—self discipline, attention to minute details, and hours of practice will make anyone a *champion*. Youngsters should supplement formal practice with workouts at home or in the residential setting, on weekends and on nonpractice days. Send suggested activities to and meet with parents or ward attendants to suggest home, cottage, or ward conditioning, running, jumping, and throwing activities. Motivate youngsters, give them status and recognition, and make them taste success. Here are some motivational tips—

		8 - 9 Years					10 - 12 Years				
		ROOKIE	WINNER	STAR	CHAMP	SUPER CHAMP	ROOKIE	WINNER	STAR	CHAMP	SUPER CHAMP
50 Yard Dash	Boys	10.7 sec.	9.9 sec.	8.9 sec.	8.6 sec.	7.2 sec.	9.0 sec.	8.3 sec.	7.9 sec.	7.2 sec.	6.6 sec.
	Girls	11.4 sec.	10.5 sec.	9.1 sec.	8.8 sec.	7.1 sec.	9.5 sec.	8.8 sec.	8.1 sec.	7.4 sec.	6.4 sec.
300 Yard Run	Boys	94 sec.	84 sec.	77 sec.	74 sec.	62 sec.	82 sec.	72 sec.	65 sec.	52 sec.	38.8 sec.
	Girls	103 sec.	93 sec.	84 sec.	79 sec.	67 sec.	88 sec.	78 sec.	69 sec.	52 sec.	41.7 sec.
Standing Long Jump	Boys	3'0"	3'10"	4'5"	4'9"	5'6"	4'2"	4'10"	5'4"	7'1"	7'11"
	Girls	2'10"	3'4"	3'9"	4'1"	5'0"	3'8"	4'3"	4'11"	6'0"	7'5"
Softball Throw	Boys	44'	58'	73'	85'	122'	76'	95'	114'	136'	197'
	Girls	22'	34'	46'	58'	98'	42'	56'	71'	102'	146'
High Jump	Boys										
	Girls										
100 Yard Dash (for Relay)	Boys										
	Girls										
One Mile Run	Boys										

Use chart as a *guide* to evaluate a youngster's relative ability and performance in each Special Olympics event. Times, distances, and heights can be used for motivational purposes, individual goals, or as a basis for team/class/squad honor roll. Make adjustments in listed times, distances, and heights according to local and state situations and levels of youngsters. In every case, make steps challenging and attainment of each level a significant accomplishment.

- Practice form, reaction, and gun starts where 50, 300, and relay actually begin to accustom youngsters to starting where competitive events begin.

- No special mention or emphasis is placed on practicing in lanes. Youngsters, whether they have difficulty or not staying in straightaway or curve lanes, need to run in lanes during most all practice sessions.

- Friday practice sessions are planned in terms of competitive efforts and activities. After the third or fourth cycle, substitute formal time trials, intrasquad meets or practice mailagraphic, telegraphic, or regular practice meets with other schools, teams, classes, or squads.

- Encourage youngsters in field events to practice form, work on drills, and go through movements while others are taking their turns or practice efforts; plan practice sessions so no time is wasted and everyone is constantly involved in constructive activity.

13 - 15 Years

ROOKIE	WINNER	STAR	CHAMP	SUPER CHAMP
8.1 sec.	7.5 sec.	7.1 sec.	6.6 sec.	6.0 sec.
9.4 sec.	8.6 sec.	8.0 sec.	7.4 sec.	6.6 sec.
70 sec.	61 sec.	58 sec.	50 sec.	34.1 sec.
90 sec.	80 sec.	72 sec.	54 sec.	40.7 sec.
5'3"	5'9"	6'4"	7'11"	10'
4'0"	4'6"	5'1"	6'3"	7'10"
111'	137'	159'	191'	253'
46'	65'	84'	111'	158'
3'	4'	4'6"	4'10"	5'2"
2'	3'	3'6"	3'10"	4'2"
14.1 sec.	13.5 sec.	12.7 sec.	11.8 sec.	11.0 sec.
15.1 sec.	14.5 sec.	13.7 sec.	12.8 sec.	12.0 sec.

16 - 18 Years

ROOKIE	WINNER	STAR	CHAMP	SUPER CHAMP
7.9 sec.	6.9 sec.	6.3 sec.	6.0 sec.	5.8 sec.
10.0 sec.	9.0 sec.	8.2 sec.	7.2 sec.	6.5 sec.
63 sec.	56 sec.	51 sec.	42 sec.	32.8 sec.
95 sec.	82 sec.	73 sec.	43 sec.	40.8 sec.
5'6"	6'2"	7'2"	8'5"	9'6"
4'1"	4'9"	5'3"	6'1"	7'9"
125'	159'	176'	230'	263'
50'	62'	81'	118'	157'
4'	4'6"	4'10"	5'2"	5'10"
3'	3'6"	3'10"	4'2"	4'4"
13.9 sec.	12.9 sec.	12.0 sec.	11.3 sec.	10.8 sec.
14.9 sec.	13.9 sec.	13.0 sec.	12.3 sec.	11.8 sec.
7:00	6:15	5:45	5:15	4:54

19 Years up

ROOKIE	WINNER	STAR	CHAMP	SUPER CHAMP
7.8 sec.	7.1 sec.	6.5 sec.	6.1 sec.	5.9 sec.
9.9 sec.	9.0 sec.	8.5 sec.	7.2 sec.	6.7 sec.
63 sec.	57 sec.	52 sec.	40 sec.	31.8 sec.
90 sec.	80 sec.	71 sec.	52 sec.	44.6 sec.
5'10"	6'6"	7'1"	8'2"	9'6"
4'3"	4'9"	5'3"	5'10"	7'4"
126'	159'	187'	216'	250'
50'	61'	84'	118'	141'
4'	4'6"	4'10"	5'2"	5'6"
2'6"	3'	3'4"	3'8"	4'
13.8 sec.	13.1 sec.	12.1 sec.	11.3 sec.	10.9 sec.
14.8 sec.	14.1 sec.	13.1 sec.	12.3 sec.	11.9 sec.
7:00	6:15	5:45	5:15	4:54

Practice Cycles 2-7 are based on—

- 10 minutes warm-up
- 10 minutes special exercises
- 20-25 minutes track event
- 15-20 minutes field event
- 5-10 minutes relays, fun activities, and warm-down.

Practice Cycles 8-10 are based on—

- 15 minutes warm-up and *Flexible Five*
- 45-55 minutes track or field event
- 5-10 minutes relays, fun activities, warm-down

- Award cardboard crests or red, white, or blue ribbons or patches for achievement, effort, or improvement.
- Let youngsters wear different color shirts, shorts, armbands, or other identifying devices as performances improve.
- Establish individual, group, or squad projects such as mileage clubs. Record, chart, or graph miles an individual, group, or total squad runs or jogs over a stated period of time. For example, set up squad goals such as 1000 miles, run from New York to Chicago or from your town to the site of the state Special Olympics. Put a map in a prominent place and mark it with colored chalk, ink, or string to indicate progress.
- Post an honor roll of youngsters who have met stipulated standards—laps run per week, times/heights/distances for events, improvement, or unusual effort and sportsmanship. When a youngster makes the honor roll a second time, place a colored star, pin, or mark next to his name; use different colors each time he makes the honor roll. Plan an honor roll with enough categories so every youngster has a realistic goal to shoot for and an opportunity to gain recognition.
- Set up a Hall of Fame to recognize particularly outstanding performances by youngsters who set Special Olympics records, win state or regional championships, or place in International Special Olympics competition.

Be resourceful and use imagination and initiative to overcome inadequate facilities and equipment. For example, if you don't have a track, run on playfields, park grounds, golf courses, cross-country courses or in gyms and halls; make your own oval around a playfield or blacktop area. Arrange to use a nearby track occasionally so youngsters get accustomed to running on a track and won't be awed by it in competition.

Study the entire track and field section before youngsters report for the first practice; review often. Get an overall view of cycles and their relationship to fundamentals and teaching activities for each event. Make adjustments in terms of times, repetitions, sets, and rest intervals to meet needs and abilities of individual youngsters.

Track and field can provide many retarded youngsters with their first opportunity to experience success and break the failure-frustration cycle. You play a vital role through Special Olympics in helping boys and girls become participants, competitors, and winners, and to shed the shackles of being passive spectators and inactive losers.

USING TRACK AND FIELD CYCLES

- Every youngster except those specifically training for the one mile run participates daily in *both* track and field events during Cycles 2-7.
- Cycles 8-10 are to prepare youngsters for primary competitive events. Participants in more then one event divide time according to events—
  √ Spend one day on one event and the *next day* on another, continuing this alternate pattern.
  √ Split practice sessions so some time is spent on each event daily; in shortening workouts do so without interfering with major emphasis in either event.
  √ Determine exact approach and procedure for each multi-event competitor according to his events and specific needs.
- Daily practice sessions in every event emphasize specific aspects of that event; recognize points of emphasis so adjustments can be made for individual youngsters. Practice regimens are vigorous, strenuous, and psychologically taxing; they are sequential, progressive, realistic, and designed to bring the best out of each participant. Since cycles are guides, not gospel, they can be modified and adapted to age, ability, condition, and interest of each youngster. Adjustments can be made by reducing number of repetitions and/or sets, and/or lengthening rest intervals and/or times of runs.
- Intervals between runs and sets consist of easy running, jogging, or walking, *never sitting or lying down*. These intervals are expressed in terms of time or distance to ensure control between runs and at the same time provide flexibility for coaches to adapt to participants and situations. Back-to-back refers to runs repeated with little or no rest interval.
- Discretion and good judgment determine whether or not to time specific workouts or parts of practice sessions; time of season, type of workout, event, and individual needs of youngsters influence when or when not to time runs in practice.
- Cycles for 50 yard dash and 300 yard run are combined; emphasize 300 as an endurance sprint to help those in shorter dash develop endurance for running trials, semifinals, and finals and prepare them to participate in the 440 yard relay.

Warm-up/ conditioning/ fitness activities	Review or teach different exercises and activities described in section on conditioning and fitness (pp. 6-40); use various patterns according to each youngster's abilities, levels of fitness, experience, and background; vary from day-to-day to ensure balanced program and to be sure youngsters become familiar with good warm-up procedures. Consider such patterns as:

- 2 minutes each of components 1-3-5-7-9 *or* 2-4-6-8-9
- 3 or 4 minutes of two or three different components making sure nine is included every practice session
- 1 minute each of components 1-2-3-4-5-6-7-8 *and* 2 minutes of nine.

Special exercises and drills	Introduce *Flexible Five* (p. 64); make sure youngster can perform one exercise before moving to next one; add a new exercise each day; use two-three minutes *daily* for every youngster after all exercises are learned.

Screening activities	Include exploratory and problem-solving locomotor, jumping, and throwing activities such as:

- Walk (run, jump, hop, skip, gallop) fast (slow, faster, slower) in straight (zig, zag, curve) lines; go forward (backward, sideward) on toes (heels, outside of feet, inside of feet); take giant (baby, scissors, loud, quiet, soft, fast, slow) steps; go under (over, around, through, across) objects.
- Jump (hop) in various ways, into (out of, over) objects;
- Include approaches and activities outlined in Cycles 1 and 2 in volleyball section (pp. 98-99).

Introduce a variety of fleeing-chasing and dodge games, tag activities, relays, and other fun things for youngsters; incorporate activities and games such as *hopscotch, red rover, Simon (Samson) says, red light.*

Devise specific activities to get an idea of youngsters' abilities, strengths, and weaknesses —

- Look for youngsters who never get caught in tag, get hit in dodge, who catch other kids easily in fleeing-chasing and other running games, who seen to run forever, and who just look fast running.
- Line youngsters up and have them run across playground, gym, blacktop area, or field as fast as they can.
- Measure and mark a 20 yard straightaway in gym, on playground, in hall, on blacktop area, or on track — start youngsters any distance from one line — 10 yards is good; have them run as fast as they can past a second line timing them only between marked 20 yards. This *Flying Twenty* is a good indicator of natural speed since it eliminates starting technique. Have an assistant or another youngster stand at first line and hold his hand above his head until runner passes that line at which time he drops hand; start watch on signal and stop it when youngster crosses second line to get time for Flying Twenty.

Have youngsters jog easily, do bending-stretching exercises, or other relaxing activities for several minutes at end of workout to warm-down and ease out of the vigorous period of exercise with a slow decrease in the intensity of activity.

	Monday	Tuesday	
Warm-up	Continue to review or teach different activities described in section on conditioning and fitness (pp. 6-40). Make sure warm-up is balanced and youngsters are challenged to increase repetitions and difficulty of all exercises and related activities.		
Special Exercises	Be sure *Flexible Five* (p. 64) is a part of every practice session for every youngster. In addition spend time on each special exercise listed, emphasizing: *Foot Plant* Bouncers (p. 71) Back-to-front (p. 69)	*Knee Action* Hill work-up (p. 69) In-and-out (p. 71)	
Track Events	20-25 min. roadwork (p. 35)	10-15 min. 50 yd. speed repeats (p. 69). Run 4 - 220's in 35-40 sec. with 2 min. or 220 between runs.	
Field Events	─────Standing Long Jump Week───── Provide a variety of opportunities for fun jumping (p. 81) including problem solving approach applied to jumping (p. 81); observe and note needs and abilities of youngsters.	Introduce fun activities such as animal imitations (p. 22), leap frog, jumping various objects (p. 81), jumping relays and games (p. 81) and review Monday's activities.	
Mile Run	30 min. roadwork (p. 35). 15 min. 50 yd. speed repeats (p. 69).	Run 4 - 220's in 35 to 40 sec. with 2 min. or 220 between runs. Repeat 4 - 220's as above after 8-10 min. 15 min. wind sprints (p. 71).	
Fun Warm-Down	Introduce basic relay concepts and teamwork with line shuttle and other types of fun relays. Finish practice sessions with easy jogging, bending-stretching, or other relaxing activities to warm-down.		

Wednesday	Thursday	Friday
Body Angle	*Arm Action*	*Total Running Form*
Tire pull (p. 69) Form running (p. 69)	Arm exercises (p. 69) Back-to-front (p. 69)	Speed repeats (p. 69) In-and-out (p. 71)
10 min. wind sprints (p. 71) 5 min. hill work-up (p. 69) 5 min. hill work-down (p. 69) Run as many 50's as possible in 5 min.	Run 2 - 440's with 4 min. or 440 between runs. Run 4 - 220's in 35-40 sec. with 2 min. or 220 between runs. Run 8 - 110's with 1 min. or 110 between runs. Run as many 50's as possible in remaining time.	Run an all out 220 Do field event portion of workout and then complete track event portion. Run an all out 220. Run an all out 110. Run an all out 50. Allow sufficient rest between runs so youngster has recovered almost fully.
Spend 3-5 min. on special abdominal exercises (p. 83). Work on getting height into jump with drills such as balloon/fluff ball (p. 83), vertical jump (p. 24), jump over objects (p. 81, p. 83). Finish with jumping relay or games.	Spend 3-5 min. on special abdominal exercises (p. 83). Work on takeoff selecting appropriate activities from chart on p. 83. Finish with jumping relays or games.	Spend 3-5 min. on special abdominal exercises (p. 83). Work on coordinated arm and leg action during preliminary part of jump; select appropriate activities from chart on p. 83. Take 6-10 all out jumps. Finish with jumping relays or games.
Run 2 - 440's as close to desired mile pace as possible with 4 min. or 440 between runs. Repeat a total of 3 sets of 2 - 440's with 6-8 min. between sets. 10 min. wind sprints (p. 71).	Run rhythm workout (p. 76) running ¾, 880, 440 all at same pace—allow sufficient rest interval to help runner hit same pace. Practice starting form and mechanics rest of practice session (p. 72).	Run an all out 880. After 10 min. run an all out 440. After 5 min. run an all out 220. After 2 min. run 2 back-to-back all out 110's. Finish practice session with continuous running.

	Monday	Tuesday	
Warm-up	Continue balanced warm-up (pp. 6-40) and see that youngsters increase repetitions and difficulty of all exercises and related activities—challenge each youngster to do his best.		
Special Exercises	Include *Flexible Five* (p. 64) daily. In addition, spend time on each special exercise listed, emphasizing: *Foot Plant* Hill work-up (p. 69) Back-to-front (p. 69)	*Knee Action* Run tall (p. 69) In-and-out (p. 71)	
Track Events	20-25 min. roadwork (p. 35)—cover greater distance faster than last Monday.	10-15 min. 75 yd. speed repeats (p. 69) Run 4 - 220's in 32-37 sec. with 2 min. or 220 between runs.	
Field Events	── High Jump Week ── Introduce high jumping concepts with center jump, side jump, jump-twist, and pick up (p. 85).	Review high jumping concepts as practiced on Monday. Introduce high kicking and lead leg drills from chart on p. 88. Finish off with 1 or 2 leg power drills from chart on p. 88.	
Mile Run	30 min. roadwork (p. 35)—cover greater distance faster than last Monday. 15 min. 75 yd. speed repeats (p. 69).	Run 4 - 220's in 32-37 sec. with 2 min. or 220 between runs. Repeat 4 - 220's as above after 6-8 min. 15 min. wind sprints (p. 71).	
Fun Warm-Down	Introduce basic relay concepts and skills involved in 440-yard relay, including carrying (p. 78), passing (p. 79), and receiving (p. 80) baton; include and devise fun activities for these purposes. Finish practice sessions with warm-down activities.		

Wednesday	Thursday	Friday
Body Angle	*Arm Action*	*Total Running Form*
Fall drill (p. 69)	Tire pull (p. 69)	Speed repeats (p. 69)
Form running (p. 69)	Back-to-front (p. 69)	In-and-out (p. 71)
10 min. wind sprints (p. 71)	Run 2 - 440's with 3 min. or 330 between runs.	Run an all out 300.
5 min. hill work-up (p. 69)		Do field event portion of workout and then complete track event portion.
5 min. hill work-down (p. 69)	Run 4 - 220's in 32-37 sec. with 1 ½ min. or 150 between runs.	Run an all out 300.
Run as many 50's as possible in 5 min.	Run 8 - 110's with 1 min. or 75 yds. between runs.	Run an all out 220.
		Run an all out 110.
	Run as many 50's as possible in remaining time.	Run an all out 50.
		Allow sufficient rest between runs so youngster has recovered almost fully.
Review high jumping concepts to make sure takeoff foot and action in air are consistent.	Review high kicking, lead leg, trail leg, and landing drills previously introduced.	Review drills, exercises, and activities that emphasize parts of form and jump most in need of practice.
Review high kicking and lead leg drills placing greater emphasis on use of arms in explosive lift.	Use 1 — 2 — 3 jump (p. 86) at easily cleared heights to emphasize form, flow, and rhythm of jump.	Introduce proper foot plant and heel bang with 1 — 2 — 3 jump drill (p. 86).
Introduce alligator pit (p. 87), sandbag drill (p. 87), and goal post drill (p. 87).		Finish with easy form jumping.
Run 3 - 440's at pace of Friday's all out 880 with 4 min. or 440 between runs.	Run 2 - 880's as close to desired mile pace as possible with 5-6 min. between runs.	Run an all out ¾.
		After 10-12 min. run an all out 880.
Run a total of 3 sets of 3 - 440's with 6-8 min. between sets.	Run 2 - 440's at same pace as 880's with 4 min. or 440 between runs.	After 6-8 min. run an all out 440.
5 min. wind sprints (p. 71).	Practice starting form and mechanics rest of practice session (p. 72).	After 5 min. run an all out 220.
		After 2-3 min. run two sets of back-to-back 110's with 2-3 min. between sets.
		Finish practice session with continuous running.

	Monday	Tuesday	
Warm-up	Be sure balanced warm-up is continued. Experiment with different warm-up patterns involving various lengths for exercises, repetitions, and combinations of activities; discuss with youngsters how they feel after different warm-up routines.		
Special Exercises	Include Flexible Five (p. 64) daily. In addition, spend time on each special exercise listed.		
	Foot Plant	*Knee Action*	
	Bouncers (p. 71)	Tire pull (p. 69)	
	Form running (p. 69)	Back-to-front (p. 69)	
Track Events	20-25 min. roadwork (p. 35) — cover greater distance faster than last Monday.	10-15 min. 100 yd. speed repeats (p. 69) Run 4 - 220's 2-3 sec. *slower* than Friday's all out 220 with 2 min. or 220 between runs.	
Field Events	─────Soft Ball Throw Week───── Emphasize fun, form, and accuracy, not distance.		
	Provide a variety of opportunities for fun throwing (pp. 89-90) including problem solving approach applied to throwing (p. 89); observe and note needs and abilities of youngsters.	Introduce fun activities such as dodge games, throwing at targets or objects, ball handling/throwing/catching relays, and improvised games like garbage man (p. 99)	
Mile Run	30 min. roadwork (p. 35) — cover greater distance faster than last Monday. 15 min. 100 yd. speed repeats (p. 69).	Run 4 - 220's in 30-35 sec. with 2 min. or 220 between runs. Repeat 4 - 220's as above after 4-6 min. 15 min. wind sprints (p. 71).	
Fun Warm-Down	Continue work on carrying (p. 78), passing (p. 79), and receiving (p. 80) baton; have youngsters work in small groups and introduce 5 man continuous relay (p. 79). Finish practice sessions with warm-down activities.		

Wednesday	Thursday	Friday
Body Angle	*Arm Action*	*Total Running Form*
Fall drill (p. 69) Hill work-up (p. 69)	Arm exercises (p. 69) Arm accelerator (p. 69)	Speed repeats (p. 69) In-and-out (p. 71)
5 min. hill work-down (p. 69) 5 min. wind sprints (p. 71) Introduce starting form and mechanics (p. 72) - 10 min. Run as many 50's as possible in 5 min.	Review starting form and mechanics. Run 2 - 440's with 2 min. or 220 between runs. Run 4 - 220's 2-3 sec. *slower* than Friday's all out 220 with 2 min. or 220 between runs. Run as many 50's as possible in remaining time.	Run an all out *330.* Do field event portion of workout and then complete track event portion. Run an all out 300. Run an all out 220. Run an all out 110. Run an all out 50. Allow sufficient rest between runs so youngster has recovered almost fully.
Spend 3-5 min. on special warm-up activities starting with easy throwing, gradually increasing distance and intensity. Introduce step pattern (p. 91) working with each youngster at his level in sequence. Spend 2-3 min. on grip drills (p. 90). Finish with throwing relays or games.	Spend 3-5 min. on special throwing warm-up activities. Review step pattern seeing if youngsters can move to next level. Throw at ½ - ¾ effort over objects (p. 92) emphasizing form. Finish with throwing relays or games.	Spend 3-5 min. on special throwing warm-up activities. Continue to review and progress on step pattern. Spend 2-3 min. on grip drills. Throw for form and accuracy using some of suggested activities. Finish with throwing relays or games.
Run 4 - 440's at pace of Friday's all out ¾ with 4 min. between runs. Run a total of 3 sets of 4 - 440's with 6-8 min. between sets. 5 min. wind sprints (p. 71).	Run rhythm workout (p. 76) starting at ¾ mile and based on ¾ mile time from last Friday. Practice finishing drills (p. 73).	Run 1 mile all out. After 10-15 min. run another all out mile. Finish practice session with continuous running.

	Monday	Tuesday	
Warm-up	Increase challenge of exercises and activities in warm-up (pp. 6-40) by changing complexity, number, and pattern of each; continue to experiment with different patterns and routines.		
Special Exercises	Include *Flexible Five* (p. 64) daily. Spend time on each special exercise listed. *Foot Plant* Bouncers (p. 71) In-and-out (p. 71)	*Knee Action* Hill work-up (p. 69) Form running (p. 69)	
Track Events	20-25 min. roadwork (p. 35) — cover greater distance faster than last Monday.	10-15 min. 100 yd. speed repeats (p. 69). Introduce concept of float with neutral-man-neutral (p. 71).	
Field Events	— Standing Long Jump Week — Review jumping mechanics and form by having youngsters jump for fun in games, relays, and similar activities and take part in drills and other exercises described on chart on p. 81.	Spend 3-5 min. on special abdominal exercises (p. 83). Work on preliminary part of jump and takeoff selecting appropriate activities from chart on p. 83. Finish with jumping relay or game.	
Mile Run	30 min. roadwork (p. 35) — cover greater distance faster than last Monday. 15 min. 100 yd. speed repeats (p. 69) — increase number over last Monday.	Run 4 - 220's 1-2 sec. *slower* than all out with 1½ min. or 150 yd. between runs. Repeat 4 - 220's as above after 3-4 min. 15 min. wind sprints (p. 71).	
Fun Warm-Down	Review and refine relay concepts and skills — carrying (p. 78), passing (p. 79), receiving (p. 80) baton; use 5 min. continuous relay (p. 79) with teams youngsters make up themselves. Finish *every* practice session with warm-down activities.		

Wednesday	Thursday	Friday
→		
→		
Body Angle	*Arm Action*	*Total Running Form*
Run tall (p. 69)	Tire pull (p. 69)	Speed repeats (p. 69)
Fall drill (p. 69)	Arm exercises (p. 69)	In-and-out (p. 71)
	Arm accelerator (p. 69)	
5 min. hill work-down (p. 69).	Take 6-8 form starts after review of starting form and mechanics.	Run an all out 300.
Review float with neutral-man-neutral followed by 2 - 150 shift gears (p. 71) with 2-3 min. or 150 between runs.	Run pyramid (p. 71).	Do field event portion of workout and then complete track event portion.
Run as many 75's as possible in remaining time.		Run an all out 110.
		Run an all out 50.
		Allow sufficient rest between runs so youngster has recovered almost fully.
Spend 3-5 min. on special abdominal exercises (p. 83).	Spend 3-5 min. on special abdominal exercises (p. 83).	Make an all out jump— take 20 additional jumps and see how many surpass initial effort.
Work on height and in air part of jump selecting appropriate activities from chart on p. 83.	Work on landing, selecting appropriate drills from chart on p. 83.	Review portions of jump in need of most practice and work.
Review takeoff.	Review takeoff and in air parts of jump.	Finish with jumping relay or game.
Finish with jumping relay or game.	Finish with jumping relay or game.	
Run 5 - 440's 4 sec. faster than pace of Friday's all out mile with 4 min. between runs.	Run ¾ - 9 sec. faster than Friday's all out effort.	Run 1 mile all out.
Run a total of 3 sets of 5 - 440's with 6-8 min. between sets.	After 10-12 min. run 880 at same pace as ¾.	After 10-15 min., using remainder of practice session, run a total of one mile using any combination of distances with running time 30 sec. faster than mile just completed.
5 min. wind sprints (p. 71).	After 5-6 min. run 2 - 440's at same pace with 2-3 min. between runs.	
	Run 2 back-to-back all out 220's.	
→		

	Monday	Tuesday	
Warm-up	Let youngsters experiment with their own warm-up patterns (pp. 6-40)—provide guidance and assistance to ensure balance and sufficient intensity according to age, ability, experience, and condition of each youngster.		
Special Exercises	Include *Flexible Five* (p. 64) daily. Spend time on each special exercise listed.		
	Foot Plant Hill work-up (p. 69) Back-to-front (p. 69)	*Knee Action* Tire pull (p. 69) In-and-out (p. 71)	
Track Events	20-25 min. roadwork (p. 35)—cover greater distance faster than last Monday.	Review float with several repeats of neutral-man-neutral followed by 3-4 150 yd. shift gears with 2-3 min. or 150 between runs (p. 71). Introduce finishing mechanics and form (p. 73).	
	⸻ **High Jump Week** ⸻		
Field Events	Review portions of high jump developed and practiced during Cycle 3; determine basic needs of each youngster.	Spend 3-5 min. on high kicking and lead leg drills (p. 88). Determine exact takeoff point (p. 86). Use 1 — 2 — 3 jump (p. 86) approach emphasizing takeoff.	
Mile Run	30 min. roadwork (p. 35)—cover greater distance faster than last Monday. 15 min. 100 yd. speed repeats (p. 69)—increase number over last Monday.	Run 6 - 220's 1-2 sec. *slower* than all out with 1½ min. or 150 between runs. Repeat 6 - 220's as above after 3-4 min. 10 min. wind sprints (p. 71).	
Fun Warm-Down	Continue to have all youngsters practice relay skills. Use 5 man continuous relay (p. 79) and other relay activities (p. 79) for fun to end practice. Remember warm-down activities; experiment with different activities and patterns.		

Wednesday	Thursday	Friday
Body Angle	*Arm Action*	*Total Running Form*
Hill work-down (69)	Arm exercises (p. 69)	Speed repeats (p. 69)
Form running (p. 69)	Arm accelerator (p. 69)	In-and-out (p. 71)
Take 6-8 form starts followed by 6-8 all out gun starts going 20-30 yards per start. Review finishing mechanics and form (p. 73). Run pyramid (p. 71).	5 min. hill work-down (p. 69). Run 4 - 220's 2-3 sec. *slower* than all out with 2 min. or 220 between runs. Repeat 4 - 220's with 5 min. between sets. Run as many 50's as possible in remaining time.	Run an all out 440. Do field event portion of workout and then complete track event portion. Run an all out 300. Run an all out 110. Run an all out 50. Allow sufficient rest between runs so youngster has recovered almost fully.
Spend 3-5 min. on high kicking and lead leg drills (p. 88). Check takeoff point—jump several times to check this point. Review trail leg drills. Jump for form (p. 87) emphasizing action over bar (p. 86).	Spend 3-5 min. on high kicking, lead leg, and trail leg drills (p. 88). Jump for form, emphasizing action over bar and landing. Use 1 — 2 — 3 jump (p. 86) emphasizing lead leg and arm action.	Do high kicking, lead leg, and trail leg drills (p. 88). Compete in time-trial jumping (p. 87). Jump for form 2-3 inches below height at which missed three times.
Run 6 - 440's 4 sec. faster than pace of Friday's all out mile with 4 min. between runs. Run a total of 3 sets of 6 - 440's with 4-6 min. between sets. 5 min. wind sprints (p. 71).	Run rapid rhythm (p. 76) workout using Friday's mile time as basis for starting time. Repeat rapid rhythm workout starting at 880 this time.	Run 1 mile all out. Run 880 all out after 10-12 min. Complete practice session with continuous run on golf course, cross country course, around building, through woods, or on track.

	Monday	Tuesday	
Warm-up	Have youngsters continue to experiment with their own warm-up patterns — emphasize balanced and vigorous warm-up (pp. 6-40).		
Special Exercises	Include *Flexible Five* (p. 64) daily. Spend time on each special exercise listed. *Foot Plant* Bouncers (p. 71). Jump rope.	*Knee Action* Run tall (p. 69). Back-to-front (p. 69).	
Track Events	20-25 min. roadwork (p. 35) — cover greater distance faster than last Monday.	10-15 min. 100 yd. speed repeats (p. 69). Run 440 overdistance (p. 71). Repeat 440 overdistance after almost full recovery.	
Field Events	Review throwing mechanics and form by having youngsters throw for fun in games, relays, and similar activities and take part in drills and other exercises described on pp. 89-93.	Spend 3-5 min. on special throwing-warm up activities and 2-3 min. on grip drills. Work on step pattern (p. 91) emphasizing form, rhythm, flow, sequence, and increased speed. Make 6-10 throws at ¾ effort. Finish with throwing relays and games.	
Mile Run	30 min. roadwork (p. 35) — cover greater distance faster than last Monday. 15 min. 100 yd. speed repeats (p. 69) — increase number over last Monday.	Run 2 - 440's 2-3 sec. *slower* than all out with 2-3 min. or 440 between runs. Run 4 - 220's *all out* with 1 ½ min. or 150 between runs. Run 4 - 110's *all out* with 1 min. between runs. Run wind sprints (p. 71) remaining time.	
Fun Warm-Down	Divide youngsters into groups of five to practice relay fundamentals (pp. 78-80) and for continuous relay (p. 79). Let each youngster warm-down in his own way.		

—— **Soft Ball Throw Week** ——

Wednesday	Thursday	Friday
Body Angle	*Arm Action*	*Total Running Form*
Tire pull (p. 69).	Hill work-up (p. 69).	Speed repeats (p. 69).
Fall drill (p. 69).	In-and-out (p. 71).	In-and-out (p. 71).
Review starting form (p. 72) and mechanics; take 6-8 form starts (p. 72) and 6-8 gun starts.	5 min. hill work-down (p. 69).	Let youngsters select 2 of following 3 events to run all out—*300, 110, 50.*
Run superduper (p. 71).	Run go-man-go (p. 71).	Run first event, complete field event, and then run second event.
Repeat superduper after almost full recovery.	Repeat go-man-go after almost full recovery.	
	Review finishing form and mechanics (p. 73).	
Spend 3-5 min. on special throwing warm-up activities and 2-3 min. on grip drills.	Spend 3-5 min. on special throwing warm-up activities and 2-3 min. on grip drills.	Make an all out throw—take 20 additional throws and see how many surpass initial effort.
Review step pattern (p. 91).	Review step pattern.	Review portions of throw in need of most practice and work.
Throw over objects at different distances (p. 92).	Throw for form (p. 92).	Finish with throwing relays or games.
Make 8-12 throws at ¾ effort.	Make 10-15 throws at ¾ effort and 3-6 all out throws.	
	Finish with throwing relays and games.	
Run 8 - 440's 4 sec. faster than pace of Friday's all out mile with 3 min. between runs.	Run ¾ 9 sec. faster than Friday's mile pace—wait 2 min. and run all out 440.	Run 1 mile all out.
After 6-8 min. run 4 back-to-back 110's all out.	After 8-10 min. run 880 6 sec. faster than Friday's mile pace—wait 1 min. and run all out 440.	After 12-15 min. run 880 all out.
	10 min. 100 yd. speed repeats (p. 69).	Run mile in pattern described for Friday in Cycle 5.

	Monday	Tuesday	
Warm-up	Have entire squad warm-up together; include easy jogging, balanced conditioning-fitness activities (pp. 6-40), *Flexible Five* (p. 64), and special exercises to help individuals. Continue to encourage each youngster to experiment with different warm-up patterns and routines according to his age, physical condition, and track/field events.		
50 Yard Dash *and* 300 Yard Run	5 min. drills emphasizing foot plant (p. 70). 5 min hill work-up (p. 69). 5 min. back-to-front (p. 69). Run 4 - 220's at desired 300 pace with 2 min. or 220 between runs. Repeat 4 - 220's with 5-6 min. between sets. 10 min. 100 yd. speed repeats (p. 69).	5 min. drills emphasizing knee action (p. 70). 5 min. hill work-down (p. 69). 5 min. in-and-out (p. 71). 10 min. on starting form and mechanics at start of 50 or 300 (p. 72). Run overdistance 440 (p. 71). Repeat overdistance 440 after almost full recovery. 5-10 min. 50 yd. wind sprints (p. 71).	
Mile Run	Run 4 - 440's 4 sec. faster than Friday's mile pace with 3 min. between runs. Repeat 4 - 440's after 5-6 min. 15 min. 100 yd. speed repeats (p. 69).	Run 3 - 880's at desired mile pace with 4-6 min. between runs. Run 4 - 440's at desired mile pace with 2-3 min. between runs. Run 5 - 220's at desired mile pace with 1 min. between runs.	
Standing Long Jump	5 min. additional abdominal exercises (pp. 18-20). 5 min. vertical jump, jump and reach (p. 24), or other power exercises. 15 min. drills and activities (p. 83) emphasizing takeoff. 10 min. drills and activities emphasizing preliminary part of jump (p. 83). 10 min. 50 yd. speed repeats (p. 69).	5 min. additional abdominal exercises (pp. 18-20). 10 min. drills and activities (p. 83) emphasizing in-air form. 10 min. drills and exercises emphasizing landing. 10 min. form jumping. 10 min. wind sprints (p. 71).	
High Jump	10 min. additional stretching, high kicking (p. 86) and trail leg drills (p. 87). 15 min. jumping at easy heights to determine needs of each jumper. Obtain exact takeoff point (p. 86) and starting point (p. 86). 10 min. 50 yd. speed repeats (p. 69).	10 min. additional stretching, high kicking (p. 86) and trail leg drills (p. 87). Check takeoff point (p. 86) and adjust. 15 min. 1-2-3 jump (p. 86) emphasizing foot plant and takeoff. 10 min. 1-2-3 jump emphasizing arm action (p. 86). 5 min. in-and-out (p. 71).	
Softball Throw	5 min. additional arm/shoulder exercises (pp. 15-18). 10 min. easy warm-up throwing. 15 min. throwing over objects (p. 92) to obtain angle of release. 5 min. grip drills (p. 90). 10 min. throw for form (p. 92). 5 min. 50 yd. speed repeats (p. 69).	5 min. additional arm/shoulder exercises (pp. 15-18). 10 min. easy warm-up throwing. 15 min. throw with emphasis on step pattern (p. 91). 5 min. grip drills (p. 90). 10 min. throw for form (p. 92). 5 min. hill work-up (p. 69).	
Fun and Relay Activities	Review mechanics of carrying (p. 78), receiving (p. 79), passing (p. 80) baton; start emphasizing timing between incoming and outgoing runners (p. 80); include 5 man continuous relay near finish of practice sessions. Consider fun relays and games too. Make sure all warm-down sufficiently.		

Wednesday	Thursday	Friday
5 min. drills emphasizing body angle (p. 70). 5 min. tire pull (p. 69). 5 min. form running (p. 69). Take 6-8 reaction starts (p. 72), and 6-8 gun starts. Run 2-3 - 125 yd. neutral-man-neutral (p. 71) with 2-3 min. between runs. Run go-man-go (p. 71). Do form running remaining time.	5 min. drills emphasizing arm action (p. 70). 5 min. hill work-up (p. 69). 5 min. hill work-down (p. 69). 15-20 min. roadwork (p. 35). 10 min. 100 yd. speed repeats (p. 69).	Run competitive 50. Repeat 2 more competitive 50's spaced as semifinals and finals. *OR* Run competitive 300. *Both events:* Discuss all parts of competitive effort. Work on parts of race in need of additional attention.
Run ¾ mile at desired mile pace. After 10 min. run 880 at desired mile pace. After 5 min. run back-to-back 440's at desired mile pace. 100 yd. speed repeats remainder of practice session.	Roadwork (p. 35) or continuous running entire practice session.	Run one mile all out. Discuss strategy, tactics, and similar phases of mile run. End with an all out 880.
5 min. additional abdominal exercises (pp. 18-20). Take 25 all out jumps to determine where best effort occurs (p. 84). Run in-and-outs (p. 71) remainder of session.	5 min. additional abdominal exercises (pp. 18-20). Roadwork (p. 35), continuous running or fun activities for rest of practice session.	Warm-up as for meet including pre-competition jumps. Take 3 competitive jumps. Take 6 more sets of 3 competitive jumps. Work on parts of jump in need of additional attention.
10 min. additional stretching, high kicking (p. 86) and trail leg drills (p. 87). Check takeoff point (p. 86) and adjust. 15 min. high bar drill (p. 86) emphasizing trail leg action and landing (p. 87). Check starting point (p. 86) and jump at easy heights from it. 5 min. 50 yd. wind sprints.	10 min. additional stretching, high kicking, (p. 86), and trail leg drills (p. 87). 15 min. extra drills including ones for each portion of jump. Time trial jumping (p. 87). Jump for form during remaining time.	Warm up as for meet. Jump as in competition, continuing 3 heights above official miss. Start at last height and use inverted jump (p. 87) drill back to original starting height.
5 min. additional arm/shoulder exercises (pp. 15-18). 10 min. easy warm-up throwing. Take 25 all out throws to determine where best effort occurs (p. 93). Run 50 yd. wind sprints (p. 71) rest of practice session.	5 min. additional arm/shoulder exercises (pp. 15-18). 10 min. easy warm-up throwing. Roadwork (p. 35), continuous running, jumping or fun activities for rest of practice session.	Warm up as for meet including precompetition throws. Take 3 competitive throws. Take 6 more sets of 3 competitive throws. Work on parts of throw in need of additional attention.

	Monday	Tuesday	
Warm-up	Continue to have entire squad warm-up as a unit but place greater emphasis on individual patterns and routines according to specific events for which youngster is preparing and in terms of special needs of track/field events themselves. Discuss with each youngster how he feels after various patterns and routines — remember, most youngsters do not warm-up enough, not too much.		
50 Yard Dash and 300 Yard Run	5 min. drills emphasizing foot plant (p. 70). 5 min. hill work-up (p. 69). 5 min. back-to-front (p. 69). Run overdistance 440 (p. 71). Run 2 superdupers (p. 71) with 3-4 min. between runs. 5-10 min. 50 yd. wind sprints (p. 71).	5 min. drills emphasizing knee action (p. 70). 5 min. hill work-down (p. 69). 5 min. in-and-out (p. 71). Run pyramid (p. 71). 5-10 min. 50 yd. wind sprints (p. 71).	
Mile Run	Run 4 - 440's 4 sec. faster than pace of season mile time objective with 2-3 min. between runs. Repeat 4 - 440's after 4-5 min. Run 4 all out 220's with 1 min. between runs.	Run rhythm workout (p. 76) based on season mile time objective.	
Standing Long Jump	5 min. additional abdominal exercises (pp. 18-20). 5 min. jump without using arms (p. 83). 15 min. jump for height (p. 83). 10 min. jump for form emphasizing spring, power, height (p. 83). 10 min. 50 yd. wind sprints (p. 71).	5 min. additional abdominal exercises (pp. 18-20). Take 25 all out jumps to determine where best effort occurs (p. 84). Run in-and-outs (p. 71) remainder of session.	
High Jump	10 min. additional stretching, high kicking (p. 86), and trail leg drills (p. 87). Check takeoff and starting points (p. 86). Jump for form (p. 86). Run 4 - 220's with 2 min. or 220 between runs.	10 min. additional stretching, high kicking (p. 86), and trail leg drills (p. 87). Check takeoff point and adjust (p. 86). 15 min. 1 — 2 — 3 jump (p. 86), emphasizing foot plant. 15 min. 1 — 2 — 3 jump emphasizing lead leg and arm action. 5 min. in-and-out.	
Softball Throw	5 min. additional arm/shoulder exercises (pp. 15-18). 10 min. easy warm-up throwing. 10 min. throwing emphasizing step pattern (p. 91). 5 min grip drills (p. 90). 10 min. throwing over objects (p. 92). 5-10 min. 50 yd. speed repeats (p. 69).	5 min. additional arm/shoulder exercises (pp. 15-18). 10 min. easy warm-up throwing. Take 25 all out throws to determine when best effort occurs (p. 93). Run 50 yd. sprints (p. 71) remaining portion of session.	
Fun and Relay Activities	Experiment with youngsters in different combinations for relay teams; emphasize working together and getting timing as units; refine mechanics of carrying (p. 78), receiving (p. 79), and passing (p. 80) baton. Include practice relays and other relay activities. Continue to stress warm-down even at this stage of program and in warm weather.		

Wednesday	Thursday	Friday
5 min. drills emphasizing body angle (p. 70). 5 min. tire pull (p. 69). 5 min. form running (p. 69). Take 6-8 reaction starts (p. 72) and 6-8 gun starts (p. 72). Work on float with either neutral-man-neutral (p. 71) or shift gears (p. 71). 5-10 min. 50 yd. wind sprints (p. 71).	5 min. drills emphasizing arm action (p. 70). 5 min. hill work-up (p. 69). 5 min. hill work-down (p. 69). 5-10 min. form starts (p. 72). 5-10 min. finishing drills (p. 73). 10-20 min. roadwork (p. 35).	Run competitive 50. Repeat 2 more competitive 50's spaced as semifinals and finals _OR_ Run competitive 300. _Both Events:_ Discuss start, form, pace finish of competitive effort. Use drills, exercises, and activities in areas in need of additional attention.
Run rapid rhythm workout (p. 76) based on season mile time objective. Repeat rapid rhythm workout starting at 880 after 10-12 min.	Roadwork (p. 35) or continuous running entire practice session.	Run 1 mile all out. Discuss pace, form, endurance, speed, and other aspects of mile run. End with another all out mile run.
5 min. additional abdominal exercises (pp. 18-20). 15 min. extra drills according to needs of individual jumpers. 20 min. form jumping emphasizing part of jump in need of extra attention. 5 min. 50 yd. speed repeats (p. 69).	5 min. additional abdominal exercises (pp. 18-20). Roadwork (p. 35), continuous running or fun activities entire session.	Warm up as for meet, including pre-competition jumps. Take 3 competitive jumps. Discuss form and other aspects of jumps. Take 9-15 more all out jumps in sets of three.
10 min. additional stretching, high kicking (p. 86), and trail leg drills (p. 87). Check starting point (p. 86), including form approach (p. 86). 15 min. high bar drill (p. 86) emphasizing trail leg action and landing. Jump for form (p. 86). 5 min. 50 yd. speed repeats (p. 69).	10 min. additional stretching, high kicking (p. 86), and trail leg drills (p. 87). 15 min. extra drills including ones for each portion of jump. Time trial jumping (p. 87). Jump for form during remaining time emphasizine parts of jump needing additional practice.	Warm up as for meet Jump as in competition continuing two heights above official miss. Start bar over and jump as in competition continuing for rest of session.
5 min. additional arm/shoulder exercises (pp. 15-18). 10 min. easy warm-up throwing. Divide entire time among drills and activities to emphasize major throwing needs (pp. 89-93). 5 min. hill work-up (p. 69).	5 min. additional arm/shoulder exercises (pp. 15-18). 10 min. easy warm-up throwing. Roadwork (p. 35), continuous running, jumping or fun activities remainder of practice session.	Warm-up as for meet including pre-competition throws. Take 3 competitive throws. Discuss form and other aspects of throws. Take 9-15 more all out throws in sets of three.

	Monday	Tuesday	
Warm-up	Emphasize premeet warm-up procedures throughout week; make minor adjustments and help each youngster know and feel when he is ready for his event. Make sure everyone knows how long he must warm-up before his event, exact number of activities and exercises to include, procedures immediately before competition, and what to do between events and before second events.		
50 Yard Dash and 300 Yard Run	5 min. hill work-up (p. 69). 5 min. hill work-down (p. 69). 5 min. form running (p. 69). Run 4 - 220's 2-3 sec. faster than 300 pace with 2 min. or 220 between runs. Run 4 - 110's all out with 2 min. or 110 between runs. Run 4 - 50's all out with 1 min. or 50 between runs. Work on finishing drills (p. 73).	5 min. form drills (p. 69). 5 min. hill work-up (pl 69). 5 min. form running (p. 69). 6-8 form starts (p. 72). 8-12 reaction and gun starts mixed (p. 72). Run 2 go-man-go (p. 71) with almost full recovery between each run. Work on finishing drills (p. 73). Run in-and-outs (p. 71) remainder of session.	
One Mile Run	Run 6 - 440's at desired pace — 2-3 min. between runs. Run 4 - 440's 4 sec. faster than pace. Run 2 back-to-back all out 440's.	Run 880 at desired pace. Repeat 880 at this pace 2 or 3 more times after almost full recovery.	
Standing Long Jump	5 min. additional abdominal exercises (pp. 18-20). 15 min. exercises, drills, practice on preliminary part and takeoff (p. 83). 15 min. exercises, drills, practice on in air and landing part of jump (p. 83). 6-12 jumps (p. 83). 5 min. 50 yd. wind sprints (p. 71).	5 min. additional abdominal exercises (pp. 18-20). Take 12-15 all out jumps to check pattern of best effort (p. 84). Jump for form remainder of session. 5 min. 50 yd. speed repeats (p. 69).	
High Jump	10 min. additional stretching, high kicking, and trail leg drills (pp. 86-87). 15 min. 1-2-3 jump (p. 86) emphasizing foot plant and arm action. 15 min. 1-2-3 jump — high bar (p. 86) combination emphasizing action over bar and landing. 10 min. jump for form 2-3" under season's best height. 5 min. 50 yd. wind sprints (p. 71).	10 min. additional stretching, high kicking, and trail leg drills (pp. 86-87). Check starting point (p. 86). 6-8 form approach (p. 86). Jump for form with full approach 2-4" under, season's best height. Move bar up 2" at a time making 3 attempts at each height, until bar is 4" over season's best. 5 min. in-and-out (p. 71).	
Softball Throw	5 min. additional arm/shoulder exercises (pp. 15-18). 10 min. easy warm-up throwing. 15 min. exercises, drills, practice on step pattern (p. 91). 15 min. exercises, drills, practice for height and angle of throw (p. 92). 6-12 form throws (p. 92). 5 min. 50 yd. wind sprint (p. 71).	5 min. additional arm/shoulder exercises (pp. 15-18). 10 min. easy warm-up throwing. Take 12 - 15 all out throws to check pattern for best effort (p. 93). Throw for form remainder of session (p. 92). 5 min. 50 yd. wind sprints (p. 71).	
Fun and Relay Activities	Divide squad/class into relay teams keeping competing units together; review mechanics as necessary; emphasize timing between runners and overall teamwork; run total relay at least once per day — start teams at different times (2, 3, 5, 10 sec. apart) to make all teams run faster. Complete each session with appropriate warm-down activities.		

Wednesday	Thursday	Friday
15 min. drills and exercises emphasizing most needed aspects of form. 6-8 *easy* form starts (p. 72). Run 2 or 3 neutral-man-neutral (p. 71) or shift gears (p. 71) to work on float (p. 70). Complete session with continuous running, roadwork, in-and-out or other easy and relaxing run.	*For All Events:* Give youngsters option to: Take day off. Warm-up, jog, run easy. Do roadwork (p. 35). Take a long continuous run. Work on some phases of form in event. Dress in uniform and take a sun bath. Do drills, exercises, and other activities to polish form in event. Participate in other events especially those involving skills and activities different from competitive event. Take part in relays, games, and other fun activities. Participate in activities of their own choosing.	*For All Events:* Have each youngster participate in events in which he will participate in competition, spaced like actual meet. Divide squad into two or three teams and conduct competition as actual meet. Invite other schools, classes, squads, centers, or agencies to participate in a practice or regular meet. Add special events or activities so each youngster has additional opportunities to participate and compete in events similar to his primary event. Let each youngster take part in his events as well as one or two additional ones of his choice.
Run ¾ at desired pace — wait 2 min. and run all out 550 yds. Repeat ¾ as above after almost full recovery.		
5 min. additional abdominal exercises (pp. 18-20). 20 min. exercises, drills, practice on portions of jump in most need of additional attention (p. 83). 10 min. jump for form (p. 83). 10 min. in-and-out (p. 71).		
10 min. additional stretching, high kicking, and trail leg drills (pp. 86-87). 20 min. exercises, drills, practice on portions of jump in most need of additional attention (p. 88). 10 min. jump for form (p. 86). 10 min. 50 yd. speed repeats (p. 69).		
5 min. additional arm/shoulder exercises (pp. 15-18). 10 min. easy warm-up throwing. 20 min. exercises, drills, practice on portions of throw in most need of additional attention (pp. 89-93). 10 min. throw for form (p. 92). 10 min. 50 yd. speed repeats (p. 69).		

FLEXIBLE FIVE

Flexibility of thighs and calves is vital to success in track and field. Therefore, special, bending/stretching and flexibility exercises described in conditioning and fitness section must be part of every track and field practice session. *Flexible Five* has been designed to give special attention to flexibility for both track and field competitors. Youngsters should do *Flexible Five after* basic conditioning and fitness activities.

- *Calf Stretcher*—stand in front of tree, fence, wall, or similar object; extend arms forward and touch object with finger tips; *keep heels flat on ground* throughout exercise; bend arms and touch chest to object; start with heels near object and *gradually* move heels away from object as calf muscles become more flexible.

- *Side Lunger*—spread legs as far apart as possible; bend left knee, keep right leg straight, and stretch inside of right thigh; reverse and stretch inside of left thigh—alternate to left and right several times.

- *Forward Lunger*—place one leg in front and other to the rear in a forward stride position; bend front knee, keep rear leg straight, and stretch back of rear thigh; reverse front and rear legs and stretch other thigh.

- *Ground Hurdler*—sit on ground with one leg straight in front of body and tuck other leg so heel is tight under buttocks; bend, stretch forward, and touch forehead (nose, chin, chest) to extended knee (ground beside extended knee); lean back and touch head to ground (back flat on ground); reverse position of legs and repeat to other side; tuck both legs under buttocks, bend back and touch head to ground.

- *Reverse push-up*—take position with hands on ground near shoulders, head touching ground, knees bent, feet flat on ground; push up as high as possible into an inverted bridge; return to starting position and repeat several times; increase repetitions as youngster gets into better condition.

RUNNING FORM

General Considerations

- Improve running form and skill by much *correct running*—running is a learned, not a natural, skill.
- Develop a style of running that is appropriate to the event—every event has requirements all its own with form unique and peculiar to it.
- Develop efficient and effective form in which all energy is expended in the race and not wasted through lost motion—incorrect form wastes valuable energy.

- Relax hands, wrists, jaw, and facial muscles—smiling requires less energy than frowning; relaxation is a key to good running.
- Learn and master all types of running form since different events require a runner to adjust form at various stages of the race.
- Practice makes perfect—good running is an accumulation of a lot of running!
- Listen while you run—a good runner should not hear himself regardless of event.

FOOT PLANT

Basic Considerations

- Land with toes pointed straight ahead, not turned in or out.
- Develop explosive drive from the track, especially in short, fast sprints.
- Use plastic heel cups if runner lands on heels or has tender/bruised heels.

50 Yard Dash and 440 Yard Relay

Land high on ball of foot—heel should not touch ground.

300 Yard Run

Land lower on ball of foot than in 50 yard dash—heel should not touch ground.

One Mile Run

Land low on ball of foot, drop to heel, and then push off ball of foot so that there is a definite *ball - heel - ball* action.

Prevent heel from slapping or hitting first; this is poor form, jars the runner's entire body, and tends to tire the legs.

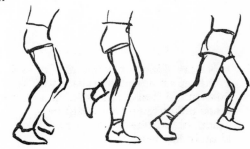

KNEE ACTION

Basic Considerations

- Remember, the shorter the distance, the longer the stride!
- Do not overstride in any event; overstriding, the cardinal sin of runners, occurs when they overreach.

- Concentrate on forward knee lift; be concerned with rear kick only when it is too high, out of line, or creates other problems; generally, appropriate forward knee lift provides the right amount of rear kick; generally the higher the forward knee lift, the lower the rear kick.

50 Yard Dash and 440 Yard Relay

Lift knee high and straight forward to develop a long powerful stride.

Use high forward knee action to obtain maximum speed and acceleration; very little rear kick.

300 Yard Run

Lift knee consciously but not as high as in 50 yard dash; stride is shorter than that of sprinter but longer than that of miler.

Use slightly lower knee action through middle portion of race; initial sprint and final kick are sprints in every sense of the word; slightly more rear kick than sprinter and slightly less than miler.

Develop a *float* during middle portion of race in which runner consciously relaxes and reaches with legs slightly more than in all out sprint. Runner should not slow down during float which is like an accelerating car that maintains speed when suddenly shifted to neutral.

One Mile Run

Lift knee slightly but not as high as in either of shorter distances; runners with small thighs can develop a higher knee action than those with heavy, thick thighs; slightly more rear kick than in 300 yard run.

BODY ANGLE AND HEAD POSITION

Basic Considerations

- Lean from ground so whole body, not just hips and waist, is involved.
- Keep head in line with rest of body since head alignment often controls body lean; do not over or under extend neck.
- Focus eyes about 12 to 15 yards in front; some sprinters may find it necessary to focus slightly closer to body.
- Use appropriate knee action for specific events to help attain proper body angle.
- Glance over shoulder if runner must look around—never turn body to look.

50 Yard Dash and 440 Yard Relay

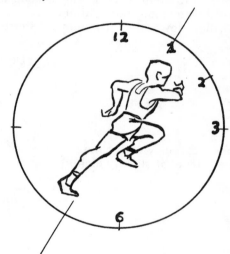

Lean between 25 and 30 degrees—about 1 o'clock.

300 Yard Run

Lean between 15 and 18 degrees—about half way between 12 and 1 o'clock.

Reduce body angle and forward lean slightly during middle or *float* portion of race.

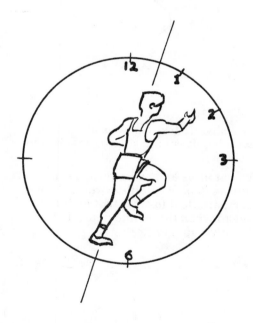

Lean about 10 degrees—about one-third of way between 12 and 1 o'clock.

Be conscious of tendency to ride back or run too straight when tired—when this happens, runner actually fights himself and reduces forward speed and momentum.

Do not look at feet of an opponent just ahead so as not to fall into his stride and cadence; focus eyes on back of opponent's neck in these situations.

One Mile Run

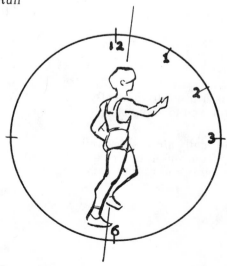

ARM ACTION

Basic Considerations

- Swing arms from shoulders—think of a pin driven through shoulder with swing from this point; backswing is generally to a point about even with plane of the back.
- Keep hands cupped, fists unclenched, and either little fingers touching palms of hands or thumbs and index fingers together.
- Bend elbows to about a right angle; keep elbows fixed throughout race; milers may carry arms further down than runners in shorter races—experiment to find best arm position for each runner.
- Swing arms relatively straight rather than across body except around turns where inside arm and shoulder are dropped and outside arm goes across body; make greater adjustments on short, sharp, tight turns so as to run as close to inside of lane as possible.
- Use appropriate arm action to help overall speed, drive, and running effectiveness and efficiency.

50 Yard Dash and 440 Yard Relay

Pump arms vigorously with hands reaching eye level or slightly higher.

300 Yard Run

Use slightly less vigorous arm action with hands coming approximately to chin level.

Lower arms and consciously relax during *float* or middle portion of race; compare float to a car that maintains speed when thrust into neutral after building up inertia.

One Mile Run

Swing arms naturally, rhythmically, evenly, and relaxed to about shoulder level.

Drop arms vertically along sides and let them hang from shoulders for a few strides to relax and reduce arm fatigue.

Running Drills and Practice Activities

There is no short cut to success in track—the only formula for success is hard work. Therefore, coaches and assistants must select challenging drills and motivating practice activities that are designed for specific purposes and at the same time are fun for youngsters. Informal activities—especially fleeing and chasing games such as *Red Rover, Uncle Sam,* and *Crows and Cranes*—tag activities, and relays can be effectively used in practice sessions. Some youngsters may lack confidence and experience in running so even in informal activities someone may have to take them by the hands and run with them. On the other hand, some may think it fun to chase another, especially the coach; others may want to be chased; still others may want to run with another person. Devise games, drills, and other approaches to make youngsters want to practice and to help individuals improve form, speed, and endurance; encourage youngsters to create their own running drills and practice activities. Use whatever approach is needed to get youngsters to run and have fun while running. Coaches and assistants are reminded to—

- Teach youngsters to think of one, and only one, aspect of form at a time; teach only one fundamental at a time—spend a few minutes on knee action, a few minutes on arm action, and a few minutes on foot plant rather than trying to concentrate on all at once.
- Make sure each youngster spends sometime every practice session on running form; strive to make good running form automatic and a habit.
- Use movies, films, pictures, and other visual aids to help youngsters see elements of good running form; demonstrate yourself and let other members of the squad serve as models.
- Use a variety of running drills and practice activities to emphasize a single element of running form; this is an effective approach to keep repetition from becoming boring.
- Be sure an ample amount of running is done in a clockwise direction so that an equal balance is maintained between right and left legs; this is especially important for runners who must go around turns.

A variety of specific running drills and practice activities can be used effectively. The following chart contains a number of drills and activities for specific aspects of running form and fundamentals.

- *Run tall*—assume appropriate body angle with arms extended and hands against a wall; run in place; start slowly to get feel of correct knee action and gradually increase speed; exaggerate knee lift as a variation to drill.
- *Hill work*—run up short (15-20 yards), steep (45-60 degrees) hills or flights of steps to develop body lean, driving arm action, knee lift, appropriate foot plant, and endurance. Run *down* long (25-30 yards), gradual (20-30 degrees) hills to attain faster leg action and rhythm than can be developed on flat surfaces.
- *Form running*—move at quarter, half, or three-quarter speed, concentrating on specific aspects of running form; have youngster think about individual elements of form as you observe and assist him. Start slowly and gradually increase speed.
- *Back-to-front*—divide youngsters into groups of five to seven; each group jogs in single file. Last runner sprints past teammates to front of line; when he has taken his place as leader, new last man sprints to front of line; continue this pattern for a specified time or given number of laps.
- *Speed repeats*—run as many 25, 50, or 100 yard dashes as possible in a specified time—5, 10, or 15 minutes; a larger number of repetitions shows increased speed or decreased rest interval, both indicators of progress.
- *Tire pull*—get in a bicycle tire with coach or teammate holding back part of tire; lean to appropriate angle against front part of tire. Get feel of this position, initiate arm action and then leg movements while still remaining in place; move down track or field, across gym or playfield while continuing vigorous sprint action. Throughout, coach or partner encourages youngster to run harder and suggests ways of improving sprinting form. During moving stages resistance is added and sprinter's forward speed is controlled by coach or partner who simply leans back.
- *Fall drill*—stand tall with feet together and arms against sides; fall forward from this position, preventing an actual fall by moving into a running position at last possible moment; maintain the angle of this position while running easily and relaxed; gradually increase speed of sprint maintaining appropriate angle.
- *Arm exercises*—stand tall with one foot slightly in front of the other, bend elbows to appropriate angle for specific event; make appropriate arm movements, gradually increasing tempo and vigorousness of motion. Introduce these same arm movements as individual walks, jogs, and runs at increasing speeds; progress to the next level as performance warrants and use these different approaches to develop efficient arm action; carry weights in hands to develop greater arm and shoulder strength and endurance.
- *Arm accelerator*—synchronize arm and leg movements while running with a partner; ac-

RUNNING DRILLS AND PRACTICE ACTIVITIES

Drill/Activity	Page	Foot Plant	Knee Action	Body Angle	Arm Action	Speed/ Leg Power	Float	Pace	Endur- ance
Run tall	69		X	X					
Hill work-up	69	X	X	X	X	X			X
Hill work-down	69					X			
Form running	69	X	X	X	X				
Back-to-front	69	X	X	X	X	X			X
Speed repeats	69					X			X
Tire pull	69	X	X	X	X	X			X
Fall drill	69			X					
Arm exercises	69				X				
Arm accelerator	69				X				
Bouncers	71	X							
Wind sprints	71					X			X
In-and-out or curves and straights	71	X	X	X	X				X
Squat jumps	71					X			
Overdistance	71							X	X
Pyramid	71							X	X
Go-man-go	71							X	X
Superduper	71							X	X
Neutral-man-neutral	71						X		
Shift gears	71						X	X	
Bicycle riding	—		X			X			X
Jump rope	—	X							
Roadwork	35	X	X	X	X	X	X		X
Inverted bicycle	26		X						
Partner push	25		X			X			

celerate arm action with no thought of increasing leg speed; leg speed increases through faster arm action; partner consciously accelerates arm action to catch up; continue for predetermined distance and continue procedure with runners taking turns initiating action.

- *Bouncers*—stand on one foot and bounce so that foot lands on ground in appropriate position for specific event; vary by bouncing on both feet simultaneously.

- *Wind sprints*—run all out—sprint full speed—various distances—20, 25, 30, 40 yards, maintaining speed and relaxed form; walk, jog slowly, or run easily between sprints; repeat sprints designated number of times or for prescribed time; vary by sprinting stipulated distance, return immediately to finish line, and sprint back to start, take brief rest before starting next pair of sprints; continue pattern for designated repetitions or time.

- *In-and-out* or *curves and straights*—run or sprint curves (in) and walk or jog straightaways (out) emphasizing various aspects of form; for variation reverse and run or sprint straightaways and walk or jog curves.

- *Squat jumps*—stand with one foot in front of the other; jump into the air and reverse positions of feet being careful not to go beyond a half-squat position; add challenge and difficulty by holding weights in hands or across shoulders.

- *Overdistance*—run 440 yards at speeds no more than four seconds slower than pace for 300. Use such workouts in early cycles, no more than once a week, and usually early in practice week. Generally, workout patterns get shorter and faster as week progresses.

- *Pyramid*—run distances of 55, 110, 165, 220, 165, 110, and 55 yards with rest intervals of 1-2-3-3-2-1 minutes or slowly jog distance just run. Pyramid workouts may or may not be timed; distances and rest intervals may vary according to individual condition and ability. Some youngsters may have to start with a pyramid pattern of 55, 100, and 55 yards. As youngsters get in better condition, pyramids can be repeated several times.

- *Go man go*—run 220 yards two to three seconds faster than race pace; wait no more than two minutes and then sprint 110 yards all out. When repeating in the same practice session, let youngster recover almost fully before next repetition.

- *Superduper*—run 300 yards two to three seconds slower than race pace and continue to a point 30 to 50 yards further; make conscious effort to sprint all out and maintain good form for the extra yards.

- *Neutral-man-neutral*—sprint to a predetermined point—60 to 125 yards depending upon individual ability and condition—at which time whistle is blown or some other signal given to indicate where to start float; continue float for 25 or 30 yards; a mark on or near track may also be used to indicate where to start float.

- *Shift gears*—run a segment of total race—150, 200, 220 yards—as in competition—sprint initial stage and float to end of practice segment.

Various other activities and exercises can be used as specific running drills or for practice.

Coaching Tips	
Problem	*Possible Solution*
• Knee action too low.	• Ride bicycle, especially up hills.
	• Run up short, steep hills or steps.
	• Use exercises such as inverted bicycle.
	• Run in place with exaggerated knee action—touch knees to palms held at increasing heights, starting at waist.
• Running on heels.	• Jump rope.
	• Run up short, steep hills or steps.
	• Use a variety of jumping and hopping activities, including games and confidence/obstacle courses.
	• Introduce bounce drills on one foot and two feet to emphasize staying on balls of feet.
	• Run on balls of feet starting in place and moving gradually into short runs at increasing speeds and for longer distances.
• Feet turn out or in.	• Adapt activities listed above with emphasis on placing feet straight ahead.
• Swinging arms across body or without vigor.	• Run in place, then walk, jog, run, and sprint, emphasing proper arm action.
	• Run with baton or small weight bar.

Bicycle riding, rope jumping, roadwork, and exercises such as partner push and inverted bicycle can add variety, challenge, and fun to track practice sessions. Develop your own drills and activities and encourage youngsters to devise their own ways of improving their running form, speed, endurance, and concepts of pace.

Track Special Fundamentals and Teaching Activities

Start

Special Olympics rules prohibit use of spiked shoes or starting blocks. Therefore, teach a semi-upright start as a *safety precaution* and to improve performances. This is important because Special Olympics runners do not have the sure footing provided by spikes, and without starting blocks they have nothing to drive against. *Do not teach a crouch start.*

Starting commands are: *Take your marks, Set,* and when all runners are steady and motionless, the *gun* is fired. Always use a gun or Scotch gun to start runners in practice to accustom them to the kind of sound used to start all running events. *Never* use a whistle or the word *go* to start runners in practice—get them used to the sound of the gun.

Fundamentals

Take your marks—take a comfortable stride position with toes of the front foot just behind the starting line; stand relaxed and breathe easily.

Helpful Hint:

- Place stronger foot foward; determine this by having youngster run and jump fron one foot; have him hop and perform other activities to help determine his stronger foot.

Set	Bang!
• Keep weight on the ball of the front foot; put rear foot comfortably behind front foot.	• Drive front foot forcefully against ground.
• Bend both knees slightly for balance.	• Bring rear foot quickly forward onto the track ahead of starting line.
• Bend forward from waist.	
• Keep arm opposite front foot forward and other arm back in usual running position.	• Thrust front arm vigorously back and rear arm forward; continue to move arms vigorously back and forth.
• Look at point just in front of starting line to keep neck relaxed.	• Accelerate into regular sprint stride as quickly as possible.

Teaching Activities

- Incorporate fast starting techniques in a variety of relays, fleeing and chasing games, shuttle activities, tag games; use innovations such as stopping and starting on various signals to help improve reactions and starting mechanics.
- Practice starting form; emphasize each segment at different times.
- Time 15, 20, 25 yard dashes to show youngster his improvement and how start influences times for short distances; record times on bulletin board to chart progress.
- Include stop and go starts in which youngster starts, sprints a predetermined distance, stops, starts again, and continues in this pattern for a designated time or number of starts or laps.
- Include reaction starts in which youngster develops reaction to *sound* of any type; concentrate on initial movements of start and reacting to starting sound; use loud sounds initially and gradually reduce to sharpen reaction to sound.
- Include all out—full speed—practice starts as part of each runner's practice regimen.

Helpful Hints:

- Use blank cartridges or extremely loud clap of Scotch gun; use a blank chamber or quiet clap to determine whether youngster is listening for gun or actually reacting to any sound.
- Introduce all out starts only after youngster has trained for several weeks and his legs are in good enough condition to withstand stress of all out starts.
- Be sure youngster has warmed up thoroughly before practicing all out starts.
- Work on all out starts early in a practice session to reduce chances of youngster pulling a muscle or suffering another injury due to fatigue.
- Restrict all out starts to one practice session a week and limit all out effort to 8 or 10 starts.
- Vary cadence when giving starting commands to reduce chance of youngster guessing or starting in a set rhythm.
- Practice starts individually and then with one or more teammates.
- Incorporate staggered starts in different sections of practice sessions such as running activities, form work, starts; practice starts where 300 yard run and 440 yard relay actually begin.
- Develop your own devices and activities for practicing starting mechanics, fundamentals, and procedures; encourage youngsters to develop their own approaches and activities.

Finish

The finish is an important but overlooked part of all running events. Teach runners to keep going at full speed through the tape and well past finish line.

Fundamentals

Take a breath about 20 yards from actual finish line.

Tuck chin to chest.

Start actual lean or lunge about 5 yards from tape.

Maintain same running form and foot action.

Thrust arms about a foot behind body; when arms are too far behind body, desired action is impeded.

Accentuate body lean naturally so that lean comes from hips and waist.

Drive through tape as if actual finish is 10 yards further down track.

Remember, a runner hasn't finished until his torso— *body* minus head, arms, and legs— crosses the line; a runner who falls before crossing finish line is not considered to have finished until his entire body is across line.

SUMMARY OF SPECIAL OLYMPICS ONE MILE RUN RULES

- This event is open only to boys 16 and older.
- Written certificates *must* be submitted by coaches to show that each competitor is well trained for the mile run; how long each has trained and the type and amount of training each has done should be included.
- Entrants in the mile may compete in one additional track or field event *other than* the 300 yard run.
- Competitors may not run two one mile races on the same day or on two consecutive days; heats or other trial procedures are not possible in meets lasting less than three days.

Teaching Activities

- Introduce concept of fast finishes through relays, shuttle activities, fleeing and chasing games, low organized activities, tag games.
- Incorporate fast finishes and breaking tape in specially devised shuttle relay in which two youngsters hold finish yarn for each team; outgoing runner may not start until incoming youngster breaks tape.
- Combine finishing practice with running in lanes; place string or yarn at various places so youngsters get used to breaking tape.
- Practice finishes at end of different drills and various running activities.
- Provide time and opportunities for youngsters to practice finishing form; do this slowly at first and gradually increase speed as skill and confidence improve.
- Place colorful markers, bleach bottles, milk cartons, traffic cones, bowling pins, coat hangers with colored cloth, string, or rope some distance beyond actual finish line to help youngsters develop concept and idea of running through or past actual finish line.
- Use specific drills to develop a strong, fast, and efficient finish—
  - ✓ *Plus 10*—have two or three youngsters finish together seeing who can break the tape with all continuing ten yards further to a second mark, teammate, or coach.
  - ✓ *Finisher*—start two sprinters 10, 15, or 20 yards from finish line and have them run together through finish; make this competitive—see who breaks tape first.
  - ✓ *Finish accelerator*—synchronize arm and leg movements while running with a partner—with no conscious thought of accelerating, see who can break tape while emphasizing good finish form.

Helpful Hint:

- Take cover off an old baseball and use twine for finish yarn.

SUMMARY OF SPECIAL OLYMPICS 50 YARD DASH AND 300 YARD RUN RULES

- The 50 yard dash is run on a track straightaway; grass infields should be used only if absolutely necessary. The 300 yard run is held on an oval track in lanes from staggered starts.
- All runners must start behind the starting line. A runner completes a race when his torso—trunk minus head, neck, and arms— crosses the finish line.

Lanes

All Special Olympics track events except the mile are run in lanes from start to finish. Some youngsters will have to be taught to stay in lanes throughout their events; all will have to practice so that they run in that part of a lane that is best for them. Basic fundamentals and planned teaching progressions can help all youngsters run in lanes.

Fundamentals

- Stay in middle of lane in events run on straightaway such as 50 yard dash and portions of each leg of 440 yard relay.

- Stay as close to inside of lane as possible when going around turns as in 300 yard run and portions of each leg of 440 yard relay; modify arm action (p. 68) to help take turns efficiently and effectively.

- Practice all events in different lanes so youngsters get used to running in inside, middle, and outside lanes.

Teaching Activities

- Follow straight lines on playground, in gymnasium, and in other play areas when participating in various fleeing and chasing games, low organized activities, relays, shuttle activities, and tag games.

- Introduce concept of moving—walk, jog, run, jump, hop, skip, slide, gallop, prance—in straight lines with and without guidelines on floor or outside area; gradually increase speed of movement through marked areas or lanes.

- Use objects such as bleach bottles, milk cartons, traffic cones, colored markers, painted lines, bowling pins, coat hangers with colored cloth, string or rope to mark lanes for a variety of fun activities and for marking lanes on track, asphalt, or other running areas to help youngsters develop ability to stay in a specified space while moving; make these wide and gradually reduce width as youngster's ability and confidence improve.

- Run short distances in lanes made by placing ropes between standards; gradually lower ropes until full distance from start to finish can be run in lane.

GUIDE FOR TIMING INTERVAL, RHYTHM, AND PACE WORKOUTS FOR 50 YARD DASH, 300 YARD RUN, 440 YARD RELAY

Goals		Practice Times				
50 Yd. Dash	300 Yd. Run	55 Yds.	110 Yds.	220 Yds.	330 Yds.	440 Yds.
5.0	30.0	5.5	11.0	22.0	33.0	—
5.2	31.4	5.75	11.5	23.0	34.5	46.0
5.5	32.8	6.0	12.0	24.0	36.0	48.0
5.9	35.5	6.5	13.0	26.0	39.0	52.0
6.4	38.1	7.0	14.0	28.0	42.0	56.0
6.8	40.9	7.5	15.0	30.0	45.0	60.0
7.3	43.6	8.0	16.0	32.0	48.0	64.0
7.7	46.4	8.5	17.0	34.0	51.0	68.0
8.2	49.1	9.0	18.0	36.0	54.0	72.0
8.6	51.9	9.5	19.0	38.0	57.0	76.0
9.1	54.5	10.0	20.0	40.0	60.0	80.0
9.5	57.3	10.5	21.0	42.0	63.0	84.0
10.0	60.0	11.0	22.0	44.0	66.0	88.0
10.5	62.7	11.5	23.0	46.0	69.0	92.0
10.9	65.5	12.0	24.0	48.0	72.0	96.0
11.4	68.2	12.5	25.0	50.0	75.0	100.0

Times expressed in seconds.
Times based on even pace; to obtain additional goal or practice times —

- For every 1 second added to 110 times, add

.4 - .5 sec. to 50	2 sec. to 220
2.6 - 2.7 sec. to 300	3 sec. to 330
.5 sec. to 55	4 sec. to 440

- For every .1 to .15 seconds added to 50 times, add

.7 sec. to 300	.5 sec. to 220
.125 sec. to 55	.75 sec. to 330
.25 sec. to 110	1 sec. to 440

ONE MILE RUN

Milers need to practice *at least* five days a week for a *minimum* of 10 weeks before competing in Special Olympics; each practice session should be *at least* 70 minutes, with 90 minutes preferred. In addition, milers should work out four to six weeks before starting these cycles. Precycle conditioning activities are for developing endurance, stamina, a love of running, and should include a variety of running activities (pp. 69-71) as well as emphasizing fitness and conditioning (pp. 6-40).

Practice cycles for milers are included with cycles for other track and field events (pp. 45-63). Cycles 2-9 detail special practice plans for milers. Cycle 1 is exploratory in nature to help determine a youngster's best event. However, once an individual is identified as a miler, concentrate on mile workouts. Additional information pertaining to meet day warm-up activities, exact pace work, and final preparations for competition is included later in this section.

Emphasis in the early part of the season should be upon amount or quantity of running, while later in the season it should be upon speed and quality of running.

Weekly practice patterns should generally emphasize—

- Overdistance and continuous running for endurance—Monday
- Interval training for endurance, pace, or speed—Tuesday
- Pace work at various distances—Wednesday
- Rhythm workouts for endurance or pace—Thursday
- Time trials intrasquad meets, play days, novelty workouts, or actual competition—Friday

Performances in time trials or related activities serve as a basis for the next week's practice. Plan a youngster's practice sessions for the next week or until he reaches the new goal as outlined below—

| | Mile Time | Average 440 yard Time | Times for practice intervals of — | | |
			440 yards	880 yards	¾ mile
Friday time	6:00	90 sec.	89 sec.	3:00	4:30
New goal	5:48	87 sec.	86 sec.	2:54	4:21
Friday time	5:28	82 sec.	81 sec.	2:44	4:06
New goal	5:16	79 sec.	78 sec.	2:38	3:57
Friday time	5:00	75 sec.	74 sec.	2:30	3:45
New goal	4:48	72 sec.	71 sec.	2:24	3:36

Rules of Thumb	Run each 440 at same speed	Run interval 440's 4 sec. faster than average 440 time in previous Friday's timed mile—this will be 1 sec. faster than average 440 time for new goal.	Run interval 880's and ¾ miles so that *each* 440 is 3-sec. faster than average 440 in previous Friday's timed mile.

The way in which a youngster paces himself in Friday's time trials or competitive mile is also important to the next week's practice pattern. Any appreciable deviation from even pace for any segment of a race—even halves as well as even quarters—provides the basis for practice the following week. For example, if—

- first half mile is considerably faster than second half mile, emphasize pace and endurance.

- first half mile is considerably slower than second half mile, emphasize pace.
- last quarter mile is considerably slower than each of first three quarters and/or runner fades in final stretch, emphasize endurance and speed.
- times for quarter miles are extremely uneven, emphasize pace.

The importance of practice sessions the week of the big meet cannot be overemphasized. Youngsters have worked hard and long to get in condition, improve endurance, gain speed, learn pace, and prepare themselves psychologically and emotionally for this important competitive effort. Just as daily practice sessions and weekly workout patterns must be developed to meet individual needs, so must final preparations during this last week. Instead of providing a practice pattern for the final week, these suggestions and guidelines are presented:

- Emphasize quality and speed rather than quantity and number of repetitions or sets.
- Be sure youngster is well rested and has lots of bounce in his legs on the day of competition; plan relaxing and fun practice activities for the day or two before competition. Some youngsters do not work out at all the day before competition—this is a highly individual matter.

- Stress desired race pace throughout this week regardless of distances milers run; complete each practice session with speed or sprint work to strengthen the finishing kick.
- Develop practice patterns to meet specific needs of each runner; several individuals preparing for the same race may have quite different practice patterns.
- Stress continually the importance of pace—leading at the end of the first or second lap is not nearly as important as being first at the end of the fourth lap.

To be successful, milers must develop endurance, speed, and learn pace; practice activities must be designed to develop and improve each of these fundamentals.

Fundamentals

Endurance

Ability to run for increasing distances and periods of time.

Remember, milers should be trained to run faster for longer periods of time.

Pace

Ability to run specific distances in prescribed times.

Remember, milers should be trained physically and psychologically to run even pace; the 6:00 minute miler runs four 90 second quarters; the 5:00 minute miler runs four 75 second quarters.

Speed

Ability to sprint, move fast, run all out.

Remember, milers become sprinters during their all out finishing kick.

Teaching Activities

Run on golf courses, cross country courses, tracks, or in parks, halls, gyms.

Use such activities as overdistance work, roadwork, hill work, back-to-front, speed repeats, wind sprints, in-and-outs, interval training, and continuous running described on pp. 69-76 .

Use rhythm approach in which two ¾ mile repetitions are run 24 sec. *slower* than desired mile pace—5:20 miler runs ¾ in 4:24, pace of 5:52 miler; follow with two 880 yard repetitions 8 sec. slower than desired mile pace—5:20 miler runs 880 in 2:48 pace of 5:36 miler; follow with two to eight 440's at desired 80 sec. pace; end with several all out sprints of various distances; use chart on p. 77 to plan this type of rhythm workout; use different distance combinations according to needs and conditions of individual runners.

Run repeats of various distances—55, 110, 220, 440, 880 yards, ¾ mile—at stipulated pace with prescribed rest between runs; use faster pace as runner improves, gains confidence, and condition.

Use rhythm approach in which stipulated pace is maintained for various distances—for example, ¾ mile in 3:48, 880 yards in 2:32, 440 yards in 76, and 220 yards in 38, all a 5:04 mile pace; adjust combinations and times to fit each miler's needs.

Use such activities as hill work, back-to-front, speed repeats, tire pull, wind sprints (pp. 69-71).

Run repeats of various distances—55, 110, 220, 440 yards—several seconds faster than mile pace.

Use rapid rhythm approach in which each succeeding distance is run at a faster pace; for example, a runner striving for a 5:20 mile runs ¾ mile in 4:12, 880 yards in 2:40, 440 yards in 76 sec., 220 yards in 36 sec., 110 yards in 17 sec., and 55 yards in 8 sec. (see chart, p. 77).

PACE GOALS

Mile Goal	¾ Mile	880 Yards	440 Yards	220 Yards	110 Yards	55 Yards
8:00	6:00	4:00	2:00	60	30.0	15.0
7:44	5:48	3:52	1:56	58	29.0	14.5
7:28	5:36	3:44	1:52	56	28.0	14.0
7:12	5:24	3:36	1:48	54	27.0	13.5
6:56	5:12	3:28	1:44	52	26.0	13.0
6.40	5:00	3:20	1:40	50	25.0	12.5
6:24	4:48	3:12	:96	48	24.0	12.0
6:08	4:36	3:04	:92	46	23.0	11.5
6:00	4:30	3:00	:90	45	22.5	11.25
5:52	4:24	2:56	:88	44	22.0	11.0
5:36	[4:12]	2:48	:84	42	21.0	10.5
5:20	4:00	[2:40]	:80	40	20.0	10.0
5:04	3:48	2:32	[:76]	38	19.0	9.5
4:48	3:36	2:24	:72	[36]	18.0	9.0
4:32	3:24	2:16	:68	34	[17.0]	8.5
4:16	3:12	2:08	:64	32	16.0	[8.0]

Times expressed in seconds or minutes and seconds.

Rule of thumb—run ¾ mile slower than pace, 880 yards at pace, and all shorter distances faster than pace (note example for 5:20 miler); apply this principle to other distance combinations according to needs and condition of individual runners.

Strategy and Tactics

Strategy and tactics are more important in the mile run than in any other Special Olympics track or field event. Milers run long enough to have time to plan and think during the race. Help every miler prepare a plan for every race and learn basic mile strategy and tactics.

Start

Move from starting line quickly and settle into race pace; review starting fundamentals and teaching activities (p. 72).

Lanes

Run as close to inside of track or pole as possible; run on right shoulder of runner in front to avoid being boxed by or caught behind others; remind youngsters that miler who runs shortest distance has best chance to win—if he runs in second lane, he runs 18 yards more than a mile! *Remember*—milers are not required to run in designated lanes.

Passing

Maintain contact with opponents so they don't get too far ahead—the closer to the finish line, the more important contact becomes; know how many runners are ahead and how much further it is to finish line; listen for opponents' footsteps and breathing as they come from behind; ward off passing opponent by consciously lifting knees and using more vigorous arm action to lengthen stride without changing basic running rhythm; pass at any time and any place on track so as not to shorten stride and fall into opponent's pace; pass quickly and suddenly to surprise opponent; try to open up some distance after passing opponent to discourage him from trying to repass.

Finish

Accelerate gradually through last lap—440 yards—trying to sprint last 100 to 125 yards; review sprint form, fundamentals, and teaching activities (pp. 65-71), and finish fundamentals and teaching activities (p. 73).

Consider occasional surprise *practice sessions* in which youngsters play volleyball, participate in volleyball field days (pp. 000-000), play softball, take a bike hike, participate in other track and field events, or do their own thing to avoid physical, mental, psychological, and emotional fatigue. Change pace of practice sessions to reduce possibility of youngsters becoming stale, losing interest, and regressing.

440 YARD RELAY

The Special Olympics 440 yard relay consists of four legs of 110 yards. Fundamentals of running are the same as for the 50 yard dash (pp. 65-68); lead-off man starts in conventional semi-upright position (p. 72). A team that learns to pass and receive a baton effectively can often gain enough yardage to win a close race even when opposing teams have faster runners! Organizing a relay team to make best use of each runner's talents is vital to the success of a team.

Relay Strategy

- Consider each runner's speed, condition, and ability to work with other youngsters in determining order in which team members run. For example —

  √ *Lead-off* — best starter, often second best runner.

  √ *Second* — slowest or least experienced runner particularly if he works well with lead-off man.

  √ *Third* — guttiest runner who is most likely to come from behind; often third fastest runner.

  √ *Anchor* — fastest runner and best finisher.

- Consider other possibilities in setting up relay teams such as —

  √ *Lead-off* slowest man, followed by next slowest second, second fastest third, and fastest anchor.

  √ *Lead-off* fastest man followed by next fastest second, second slowest third, and slowest anchor.

  √ *Lead off* fastest man and anchor second fastest particularly if he is strong finisher.

  √ *Run fastest* man in second position so that he often runs against slowest members of other teams.

  √ *Run on a man-to-man* basis when abilities and weaknesses of other teams are known so that specific men are matched against each other.

A perfect pass occurs when both runners are traveling at the same rate of speed at the time of exchange; it utilizes —

√ speed of both runners
√ full length of both runner's arms
√ full length of baton

Running with Baton

Use same running form as for 50 yard dash (pp. 65-68).

Maintain good arm action at all times; if baton hinders arm action, practice running carrying baton.

Keep a firm grip on baton when carrying it; however, grip should not be tight since this causes arm muscles to tense up and leads to general tieing up throughout body.

Carry baton at back end with forward end sticking out between thumb and index finger.

Pick-up a dropped baton as quickly as possible and continue race; if baton is dropped in an exchange zone, either runner may pick it up; if dropped outside an exchange zone, runner who dropped it must pick it up.

SUMMARY OF SPECIAL OLYMPICS 440 YARD RELAY RULES

- This is an *open* event with one race for girls and one for boys; ability and speed, not age, determine composition of each relay team.

- Each of four competitors runs legs of 110 yards.

- Relay begins in lanes from a staggered start; members of all teams must remain in their assigned lanes throughout race.

- Take-over or baton passing zone is 22 yards; actual exchange of baton must take place in this zone.

- Baton must be handed, not thrown, to next runner; throwing baton is a violation and results in disqualification.

- Dropped baton must be retrieved by team member who drops it unless both runners are in passing zone in which case either runner may retrieve baton.

Fundamentals

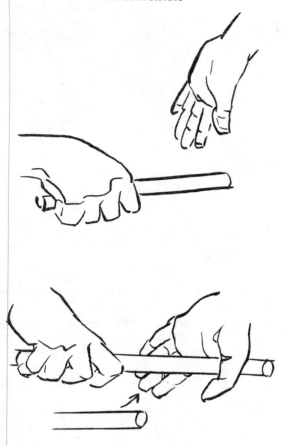

Carry baton in *right hand* and place it in left hand of outgoing runner.

Continue vigorous arm action until about two steps before passing baton; pass baton up with an underhand snap into outgoing runner's hand.

Focus eyes on V between outgoing runner's thumb and index finger.

Allow outgoing runner to take baton; continue to run hard so as not to lose valuable time during actual exchange.

Run to inside of own lane throughout race and especially during actual exchange.

Stay in own lane so as not to interfere with any other runners; move to get off track when lanes are clear of other runners.

Call or yell to outgoing runner if he is moving away so fast that pass cannot be completed in exchange zone; use *wait*, *slow down*, *easy* or other prearranged words for this purpose — this is only time runners should use verbal signals.

Teaching Activities

- Carry baton during conditioning and specific running portions of practice.
- Introduce relay concepts through a variety of line and shuttle relays.
- Use cross-field relays to reinforce relay concepts, mechanics, and techniques.
- Introduce relay concepts in activities where passing, carrying, or transferring objects are not necessary; add various objects to relay activities as youngsters gain skill, ability, and confidence.
- Divide youngsters into groups of five with numbers 1 and 5 at the starting point; position numbers 2, 3, and 4 one-quarter, one-half, and three-quarters of way around track or improvised running oval — 1 passes to 2, 2 to 3, 3 to 4, 4 to 5, 5 to 1; continue this pattern until baton has gone 5, 10 or 15 laps; this is an excellent activity to use at end of practice.
- Plan intrasquad relay meets to include regular and medley relays with legs of varying distances.
- Use hand touch or slap instead of baton to introduce relays on track or around oval.
- Work on fundamentals of carrying, passing, and receiving baton; increase speed and tempo of exchanges to race speed as youngsters gain experience and achieve timing, rhythm, and continuity.
- Have some relay work in every practice session especially in fun ways at end of workouts.
- Plan specific opportunities for competitive relay teams to work together to perfect timing and help youngsters become aware of each other's moves; master mechanics and timing of exchange; establish trigger or starting point for each outgoing runner; adjust trigger points according to weather conditions and individual runners.

Helpful Hints:

- Consider blind or nonvisual pass for teams that can master these more difficult techniques and mechanics; refer to any good book on track and field for information on this pass.
- Consider alternating passes for teams that can handle this more *difficult* procedure where same hand is used to receive, carry, and pass baton; for example — lead-off runner carries and passes baton with right hand; second runner receives, carries, and passes with left hand; third runner receives, carries, and passes with right hand; anchor runner receives and carries with left hand; less flexibility is afforded positioning runners when this approach is used.

Receiving Baton

Take position with left foot back and heel just inside restraining line; point toes straight down track.

Place right foot forward with heel slightly in front of toes of left foot; point toes straight down track.

Take a semicrouch position as if bending over to pick up a stone or other object.

Look over left shoulder and watch incoming runner as he approaches exchange zone.

Move left foot forward first much like starting any running event (p. 72); work to develop a semicrouch position that will ensure a quick start.

Extend left arm back with elbow and wrist straight.

Position palm of hand so it faces incoming runner.

Place thumb and fingers of left hand diagonally down with thumb toward outside edge of track.

Form V with thumb and fingers of left hand, keeping four fingers together.

Keep wrist straight with V belt high.

Hold hand, wrist, and arm steady as target for incoming runner.

Continue to watch incoming runner until he passes prearranged or trigger point on track when outgoing runner starts to run, accelerating as quickly as possible.

Grasp baton securely and take it from incoming runner — *never grab baton.*

Continue to look at incoming runner and baton until having secure and sole possession of baton; turn head forward and go-man-go!

Time pass so actual exchange takes place between 19 and 20 yards from incoming restraining line in a 22 yard zone.

Change baton from left to right hand on first step.

Slow down only if beyond 15 yard mark in passing zone and incoming runner cannot complete exchange in zone; ease up and wait — it's better to wait than foul and be disqualified.

Upon the fields of friendly strife are sown seeds that in other days, in other fields will bear fruits of victory.

Douglas MacArthur

JUMPING: STANDING LONG JUMP AND RUNNING HIGH JUMP

Before a youngster can compete in the *standing long jump* or *running high jump*, he must understand what jumping is all about and be able to jump. To determine whether a youngster knows how to jump, ask him to jump for fun; if youngsters don't get the idea of jumping, demonstrate for them; if they have trouble, jump up and down with them—take their hands, if necessary. Try basic jumping activities with them—

- Jump up and down with or without assistance.
- Jump the brook—jump distance between two ropes, boxes, handkerchiefs, coins, or lines on floor.
- Place a coin, handkerchief, or rope on floor—jump over.
- Set up alligator pit—jump from boxes, chairs, benches, stools, steps, ramps, or springboards onto mats, foam rubber, sawdust, or other soft landing material.
- Place bicycle tires, rope maze, or rope, wooden, or aluminum straight ladder on floor, grass, or blacktop area—jump from point to point through maze, or from tire to tire in any sequence; paint objects on floor or blacktop area; use floor tiles, cut rug runners or contact paper and place in different patterns for jumping.
- Mark hopscotch court on floor or blacktop area—jump from square to square in designated or creative patterns.
- Jump over ropes, boxes, tires, traffic cones, milk cartons, bleach bottles to experience going over an object; raise height of objects as skill and confidence increase.

- Set up novelty box and/or tire course—jump off boxes or tires, into them, over them, in original and creative ways, and in various combinations; set up challenge or obstacle course using various combinations of listed objects.
- Put bounce boards—⅛ to ¾ inch plywood, 18 to 24 inches wide, and four, to six feet long, supported on 2 x 4's or automobile tires or inner tubes—on floor and jump on them to get feel of going up in air and landing.
- Jump on a trampoline, springboard, or inverted life raft.
- Do a series of vertical jumps or jump and reach activities (pp. 24-26).
- Use a problem-solving approach—ask youngsters such questions as—
  - ✓ How high (far) can you jump?
  - ✓ How close can you get your head to the ceiling? Can you get it closer to the ceiling?
  - ✓ Can you jump over this handkerchief? Now (after moving it further away)?
  - ✓ Can you jump from this tire to that one?
  - ✓ How many jumps does it take you to go from this line to that? All the way across the room?
  - ✓ Can you jump without bending your arms?
  - ✓ What happens when you bend your knees and jump? Bend them more?
  - ✓ What happens when you swing your arms back and forth very hard before jumping?
  - ✓ Can you bend your knees a lot and swing your arms hard as you jump?
  - ✓ What can you do to jump further (higher)?

SUMMARY OF SPECIAL OLYMPICS STANDING LONG JUMP RULES

- A hard or soft surfaced mat marked with a takeoff line and long enough to cover starting and landing areas is used for competition.
- Toes must be behind takeoff line at start of actual jump.
- A *two-foot takeoff* must be used; competitors may rock backward and forward, lifting heels and toes alternately, but may not lift either foot off the ground.
- The best of three jumps is recorded in competition.
- Jumps are measured from takeoff line to closest impression on mat made by any part of body, including arms or hands.

SUMMARY OF SPECIAL OLYMPICS HIGH JUMP RULES

- Competitors must be 13 or over to participate in the high jump.
- *Takeoff must be from one foot.*
- Any jumper may, at his discretion, start to jump at the starting height or any subsequent height; three consecutive misses or failures, regardless of height(s) at which they occur, eliminate a jumper from competition—he is then credited with last height he successfully cleared.
- Knocking bar off supports or touching ground beyond plane of uprights with any part of body without clearing bar counts as a miss or failure.

Standing Long Jump Fundamentals

Preliminary

Takeoff

In Air

Place feet several inches apart with toes pointed straight ahead and just behind takeoff line.

Select an object such as a corner of a classroom, light, spot on a wall, limb of a tree, corner of a swing set, or piece of playground apparatus as a visual target to aid jumping at 45 degree angle.

Keep head down to relax neck.

Bend and stretch knees several times while swinging arms back and forth.

Bend knees, extend arms back, and shift weight to lower part of balls of feet.

Keep shoulders square with takeoff line; point toes straight ahead so as not to lose distance by toeing in or out.

Push-off vigorously from take-off mat; swing arms to gain power and propel body upward and into space; raise eyes and look at target — jump at a 45 degree angle.

Use every part of body in lift — thrust arms vigorously up, lift head and chest high, keep chin up, and arch back to aid in lifting hips.

Tuck legs and move feet forward when they are completely off ground; continue to tuck legs as midflight is reached — let feet trail body at height of jump.

Extend arms forward, curve back, spread feet apart, bend knees slightly, and start to move legs forward at height of jump.

Use movement or action in air to promote aerial balance, aid in lifting feet, and facilitate a better landing — once a jumper is in air, nothing can increase his power or lift.

Landing

Stay in air as long as possible — the longer the flight the better the jump.

Extend legs to keep entire body from dropping too soon.

Drop chin to chest, bend knees, thrust arms down and back, and keep buttocks low; keep entire body behind feet as they contact ground.

Land with feet parallel and as high on toes as possible — don't lose distance by turning while landing or by landing with one foot forward and one back.

STANDING LONG JUMP TEACHING ACTIVITIES

	Prelim- inary	Take- off	In Air	Land- ing
Hold beanbags, bowling pins, batons, bleach bottles, or similar objects in both hands and swing arms back and forth; see how many times and at what cadence (fast, slow, rhythm- ically) objects can be swung; swing arms back and forth in preliminary long jump movements.	X			
Stand and swing arms back and forth in preliminary long jump movements.	X			
Swing arms and bend knees while leaning forward and placing weight on balls of feet.	X			
Jump and bounce on both feet; hop on one foot and then the other.		X		
Assume half knee bend or squat position and bound up and out swinging arms; use animal imitation activities such as bunny hop, kangaroo jump, frog hop; include fun activities such as leap frog.		X		
Jump on tires, bounce boards, inverted life raft, springboard, trampoline to develop leg power.		X		
Jump with weight belt or jacket, carry weights in hands.		X		
Jump without using arms; do single jump, series of four or five jumps.		X		
Do vertical jump and jump and reach activities (pp. 24-26); jump and touch top of head to basketball net or get head (eyes, chest) above mark on wall, or specific object such as swing set bar.		X		
Perform standing high jump over bar or rope in long jump position.		X	X	X
Tie a balloon, fluff ball, or finish yarn to high jump standards or in some other way over long jump area—touch object or break yarn with head or chest.		X	X	
Jump over arms of another youngster or yarn, rope, or poles held by others at various heights and distances from takeoff; jump from one tire to another gradually increasing distance be- tween them; jump over different objects placed at various distances from takeoff.		X	X	
Stand near basketball backboard and throw volleyball lightly off backboard—line two or three youngsters up one behind another and have them take turns jumping as high as they can to hit ball; make a game of it to see who can hit ball most times.		X		
Have two persons hold jumper under arms while he goes through arm and leg movements.			X	
Hang onto parallel, horizontal, or stall bars, or similar apparatus to go through arm, leg, and body movements.			X	
Jump from boxes, chairs, benches, springboards.			X	X
Jump emphasizing form—*stress one aspect of each of basic components of form at a time;* Work on it for a few minutes or certain number of jumps and then change to another aspect of the same or another component.	X	X	X	X
Develop abdominal strength with sit-ups, V-ups, curls (pp. 18-20).				X
Adapt basic jumping activities (p. 81) according to interest, age, and abilities of youngsters.	X	X	X	X
Devise races, relays, and games involving specific aspects of each of basic components or total jumping action. For example, jump from one point or object to another in fewest jumps. See which team can cover greatest distances with each youngster taking one (two, three) jump(s)—each youngster jumps from point previous youngster lands. Use jumping in- stead of running in fleeing-chasing games, tag, and similar activities.	X	X	X	X

Competitive Preparation

- Make an all out jump—take three (5,10,15, 20, 30) additional jumps and see how many surpass initial effort.

- Determine when each youngster obtains his best jump. The number of jumps in competition does not permit most jumpers to achieve their best performances—they must work up to best jumps through all out practice jumps; determine this in practice as follows—

  √ Take 20 - 25 all out jumps after thorough warm-up.

  √ Record, chart, or graph each jump in terms of actual length or how much each jump increases or decreases compared with first effort—note pattern and when best jump occurs.

  √ Repeat this procedure several times—*never more than once a week*—until pattern is established whereby best jump occurs within one or two jumps.

  √ Plan premeet practice so best jump occurs on *second* of three competitive jumps. For example, if a youngster's best jump occurs on his 12th effort, he should take 10 all out practice jumps before his first competitive jump; in this way his 12th all out effort is his second in competition.

- Develop premeet warm-up pattern that includes easy running, much bending and stretching, some practice of basic jumping components, and the needed number of *all out* practice jumps.

- Compete against other members of the squad or class or in practice meets against other teams or schools; make intrasquad or practice meets as similar to actual competition as possible.

High Jump

General Considerations

- Include lots of additional stretching exercises before starting any jumping/kicking drills, practice activities, or all out jumping; refer to *Flexible Five* (p. 64), and stretching/bending (pp. 10-12), and flexibility (pp. 12-15) sections.

- Do lots of jogging, running, and sprinting to condition legs for rigors of high jumping; incorporate these activities throughout the year.

- Develop consistent and even strides so important in high jump approach through such activities as running long jump, hurdles, triple jump.

- Do lots of rope jumping.

- Use special rocker drill—place heels on a 2 x 4, curb of a track, brick, or similar object, with toes on ground, then lift toes up and down in rocking motion to stretch heel tendons.

- Adjust bar for practice jumping according to needs—put at lower heights to concentrate on form; put at heights slightly under best previous efforts to concentrate on lift; put at competitive heights to stress all out effort.

- Do not jump too much in any single practice or during any week, especially when time for competition approaches—plan practices to develop and maintain maximum spring and bounce in legs for competition.

Approach

Fundamentals

Helpful Hint:

- Experiment to find most effective approach angle since each jumper has an angle that is best for him.

Approach bar between 30 and 45 degrees, always along same line, and straight from starting point to takeoff.

Develop a seven-step approach—one long enough to generate sufficient speed yet not so long as to adversely affect speed and timing.

Increase speed of approach gradually as confidence and skill improve; control speed so as to convert as much forward motion as possible upward.

Run relaxed with a bouncy stride that accelerates from start to finish.

Lengthen final two or three strides so last step is very long, lowers center of gravity to gather (dip) or prepare body for upward explosion, and brings jumper down on his heel; *bang* heel hard against ground and keep in line with run.

Keep head and chest up and back arched during run; keep shoulders perpendicular to line of run; focus eyes over a tree, building, corner of room, light, or similar object to help lifting action.

Prevent heel bruises by wearing plastic heel cups inside socks.

Teaching Activities

Center jump—put bar (hold rope) on ground or at low height; line group up in front of bar, have each youngster run straight to bar, and jump over it, taking off on one foot; observe and note foot each youngster uses for takeoff; repeat several times so each youngster will be successful and to make sure each takes off from same foot consistently.

Side jump—send all youngsters who takeoff on left foot to left side of bar (rope) and all who takeoff on right foot to right side of bar; have each youngster run to bar and jump over it emphasizing takeoff from inside foot—left for those coming from left side and right for those coming from right side; use chalk, tape, or draw line to help with direction and approach angle.

Jump and twist—perform same jumping movements as in *side jump*—while in mid air twist or turn to land facing original starting point.

Pick-up—perform same jumping movements as in *jump and twist*—reach for and pick up handkerchief, coin, or similar object placed on floor, in pit, or on mat six inches beyond bar.

High kicker—perform same jumping movements as in *side jump*—stress vigorous kick of lead leg; combine various jumping movements at increasing heights emphasizing good jumping form and mechanics.

Takeoff point—stand next to bar with fingers of inside hand extended; use knuckles of closed fist if arms are extremely long; mark takeoff point and kick lead leg to make sure point is correct—make slight adjustments as necessary.

Starting point—get takeoff point, turn around at this point and run seven steps exactly same way as if approaching bar; continue past seventh step so as not to make an abrupt stop; mark spot of seventh step; practice approach adjusting to weather conditions, type of takeoff, condition of jumper, time of season.

Wall jumping—mark angle of approach and distance from starting point to takeoff near a wall; take regular or shortened run (1, 2, 3 steps) and approach wall—obtain maximum vertical takeoff lift so as not to hit wall.

Form approach—practice complete approach and run emphasizing such things as run, accelerated and lengthened steps, gather (dip) of body, heel plant, position of arms, head position, and coordinated approach from start to finish.

Step checks—practice complete approach and run, stress hitting takeoff point; make this as much like actual jumping as possible without attempting to clear bar.

Up and Over

Fundamentals

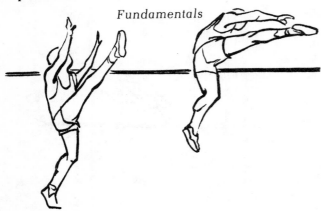

Kick lead leg upward—not forward—in direction of far standard so it is nearly parallel to bar; kick as high as possible before rear leg actually leaves ground.

Use powerful rocker motion from heel to ball of foot; drive hard and explode from plant foot—get every available ounce of lift.

Use lead leg, arms, head, and eyes to aid total lift; get hips and waist at belly button level as high in air as possible.

Thrust arms vigorously upward to aid lift; move inside arm straight up.

Start to turn body *only* after head and shoulders have gone above bar, ideally at peak of jump.

Keep arm and elbow nearer bar close to body so as not to catch bar between arm and body.

Turn head and look toward starting point to help keep body away from bar.

Rotate outside shoulder toward bar to help raise hips and aid clearance of trail leg.

Point toe of trail foot to sky or ceiling for conventional landing, *or* rotate body 180 degrees to carry trail leg away from bar for landing on back or in seated position. *Note: This is not an active kick or thrust.*

Teaching Activities

Punter—kick lead leg over head; hold hands together in front of body at shoulder level (chin, nose, eye, head, fully extended over head) and kick lead leg vigorously and forcibly to touch hands.

Loose shoe drill—loosen laces of lead foot shoe and kick; observe angle at which shoe leaves foot which indicates direction and angle of kick; the closer to 12 o'clock, the better the kick.

Belt buckle spring—approach bar with regular or shortened run and use regular takeoff. Get belt buckle as high above bar as possible.

Handkerchief drill—tie handkerchief to middle of bar; approach bar with regular or shortened run and use regular takeoff—touch toes of lead foot to handkerchief or get heel as high above this level as possible.

Vertical jumps or jump and reach - see pp. 24-26.

Cross bar clearance—place one end of bar three feet off ground and lay other end on ground; straddle bar with both feet on ground and practice various methods of getting trail leg over bar.

Standing long jump—emphasize forward thrust of arms in standing long jump to develop, improve, and refine use of arms in high jump; jump without using arms to develop leg spring and power.

One-two-three jump—start one, two, or three steps from takeoff—emphasize various aspects of takeoff, lift, and action in air.

Form jumping—use entire jumping motion and action at lower, easier heights—concentrate on specific aspects of form.

High bar drill—raise bar two or three inches higher on side trail leg will clear—right side of bar when approaching from left—jump repeatedly with one standard higher than other.

Fundamentals

Land on one or two hands and one foot *except* jumpers who land on back or in seated position.

Relax, fall into pit, and give with landing regardless of style to reduce jarring.

Cover as little distance as possible from takeoff to landing—best high jumps provide maximum height and minimum length; emphasize propelling body up not out for distance as in long jump.

Alligator pit—jump from a ladder, chair, box, or similar object onto foam rubber or mats or into sawdust; jump from increasingly greater heights; place ladder or other object at jumping pit.

Sand bag drill—lie on sand bags around jumping pit, on floor, mats, or at edge of pit; extend trail leg vertically so toe points to ceiling or sky; move from layout position through pointing stage and into pit.

Goal post—hold onto a football goal post or place hands against a wall or fence, or take another youngster's hand—extend trail leg backward and upward as far as possible to develop flexibility in trail leg; perform drill holding onto post of bed.

Activities for Total Jump

Inverted jumping—place bar four inches higher than best previous successful jump—jump to clear this height; take three trials at this height and then move bar *down* one inch at a time taking three trials at each new height.

Time trial jumping—place bar low enough to be easily cleared; raise bar one inch at a time until maximum height is reached; continue one or two inches above height at which three misses occur.

Form jumping—practice complete jump emphasizing smooth, coordinated, and rhythmic action; place bar low enough for jumper to concentrate on form.

Competitive preparation—take regular premeet warm-up including easy running, much bending and stretching, lots of high kicking, and actual practice jumps; place bar at starting height for coming meet; jump as in competition, moving bar up in same pattern as for coming meet and under actual rules governing successful and unsuccessful trials; practice two or three inches under height at which three misses occur; have two or more youngsters jump against each other as in actual competition.

Helpful Hints:

- Place bar six to eight inches above best previous successful jump during warm-up and for certain drills and practice activities so competitive heights seem even lower.

- Incorporate interesting, motivating, and challenging modifications of drills and practice activities such as jumping a specific number of times, successful or not, at designated heights, taking as many jumps as possible within a specified time.

- Finish every jumping practice session with one or two successful jumps.

HIGH JUMP DRILLS AND PRACTICE ACTIVITIES

Drill/Activity	Page	Leg Power	Approach	Take-off	Foot Plant	Lead Leg	Arm Action	Over Bar	Trail Leg	Landing	Total Jump
Center jump	85			X							
Side jump	85		X	X							
Jump twist	85							X			
Pick-up	85							X		X	
High kicker	85					X					
Takeoff point	86			X							
Starting point	86		X	X							
Wall jumping	86		X	X	X	X	X				
Form approach	86		X	X							
Step checks	86		X	X	X						
Punter	86					X					
Loose shoe drill	86					X					
Belt buckle spring	86	X				X	X				
Handkerchief drill	86					X	X				
Vertical jumps	24						X				
Cross bar clearance	86							X	X	X	
Jump and reach	24	X					X				
Standing long jump	86	X					X				
One-two-three jump	86	X			X	X	X	X	X	X	
Form jumping	86		X	X	X	X	X	X	X	X	X
High bar drill	86								X	X	
Alligator pit	87									X	
Sand bag drill	87								X		
Goal post	87								X		
Inverted jumping	87										X
Time trial jumping	87										X
Competitive preparation	87										X

Drills to Correct Common Errors

Problem	Drills
Approach too long, short, fast, slow, or at improper angle.	Remeasure seven steps, (p. 86); practice approach so jumper controls speed throughout run; experiment further with angle; use wall jumping, form approach, step checks, (p. 86).
Takeoff too close or far from bar.	Check takeoff point, (p. 86); recheck approach, (see above).
Foot plant not in line with run; failure to bang heel on foot plant.	Concentrate on foot plant in drills; check approach and takeoff point; use well jumping and one-two-three jump, (p. 86), emphasizing plant.
Lead leg kick offline or not high enough.	Use wall jumping and high kicker, (p. 85), punter or loose shoe drill, belt buckle spring, handkerchief drill, vertical jumps, jump and reach, one-two-three jump, form jumping (p. 86).
Failure to use arms in lift.	Use vertical jumps, jump and reach, standing long jump, one-two-three jump, form jumping (p. 86).
Insufficient height, lift, power.	Use wall jumping, (p. 86), belt buckle spring, hnadkerchief drill, vertical jumps, jump and reach, one-two-three jump (p. 86).
Trail leg not clearing bar.	Use high bar drill, cross bar clearance, (p. 86), sand bag drill, goal post, (p. 87), and form jumping at low heights.

SOFTBALL THROW

The softball throw for distance requires arm and shoulder power and coordination of arm, leg, and body movements. Therefore, it is important to condition youngsters before introducing them to activities involving all out throwing. Review section on conditioning and fitness (pp. 6-40), especially activities dealing with muscular endurance of arms and shoulders and leg power. Some youngsters may be completely unfamiliar with throwing activities so that *ball familiarization activities* in the volleyball section (pp. 97 - 109) will be appropriate for them. This exploratory approach can be expanded to give youngsters opportunities to experiment and explore additional movement problems with balls, beanbags, fluff balls. Different questions can be asked and many problems posed to determine a youngster's ability to handle and throw a ball:

- What can you do with a ball?
- How many ways can you throw (roll) a ball?
- Can you roll the ball, run around it, and pick it up?
- How high can you toss the ball? Can you toss the ball high and catch it high (low, near the ankles)?
- How many times can you bounce the ball without missing?
- Can you bounce it with one hand? In a tire?
- Can you stand in a tire (on a balance beam) and bounce the ball?
- Can you toss (throw) the ball off the wall and catch it? Move further back and still catch it? Still further?
- Can you bounce the ball over a line? To a partner?
- Can you toss (throw) the ball back and forth with a partner?
- Can you bounce the ball on the floor to a partner and have him catch it? Can you make it bounce twice before it reaches him?
- Can you step with your right foot and throw with your right hand? Step with your left foot and throw with your left hand? Step with your left foot and throw with your right hand? Which is easiest for you?
- Can you throw the ball to the fence (wall, tree, barrel, target)? How can you make the ball go further?
- Can you throw the ball over the football goal post (wall, tree, target)? What happens when you throw it higher?
- Can you throw the ball and hit that target?

Use games, relays, and fun activities that involve handling, throwing, and catching balls. Dodge games, activities involving throwing at targets or objects, over and under relays, and improvised games (see garbage man, p. 99) are helpful in introducing ball and throwing activities. Devise your own questions, problems, games, relays, and fun activities according to needs of youngsters with whom you work.

Consider these factors when teaching the softball throw:

- Work youngsters up to the competitive throwing stage slowly.

- *Do not ever permit youngsters to throw hard or far before they are completely warmed up.*

- Throw beanbags, fluff balls, and other light objects easily and never hard—throwing these hard could cause arm strain.

- Use simple and fun activities for warm-up—

  ✓ Throw a ball against a wall and catch it—start a few feet from the wall and gradually move back.

  ✓ Play catch with a partner—throw easily and gradually move back.

The rest of this section deals with *fundamentals* and *teaching activities* for throwing grip, preparing to throw, and throwing. Considerations for competitive preparation are also included. Regardless of a youngster's ability, there are activities, methods, and approaches suitable for him. A final reminder—over throwing in practice can lead to a tired or injured arm; softball throwers need to be fresh; their arms require lots of whip and zip.

Throwing Grip

Descriptions are for right handed throwers—reverse for left handers.

Fundamentals

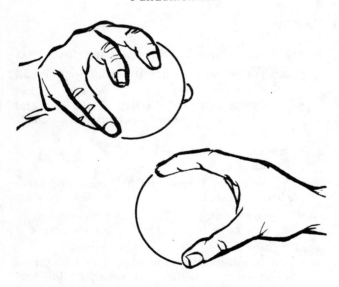

Place first and second fingers—those nearest thumb—on top of ball and spread them slightly; put thumb under ball; place third and fourth fingers on side of ball.

Hold ball on fingertips, not in palm of hand.

Helpful Hint:

- Realize that youngsters with small hands may place all four fingers on top of ball, thumb to one side, and hold ball in palm of hand.

Teaching Activities

- Grip beanbags, fluff balls, tennis balls, various size playground balls, and regulation softballs for practice; experiment with different balls to strengthen fingers, develop finger dexterity, get feel of conventional grip, and determine most effective grip for each individual.

- Place ball in front of youngster, have him pick it up, and grip it as quickly as possible; make it a game, relay, or other fun activity.

- Squeeze soft rubber ball, tennis ball, hand grips, or similar objects to develop finger, hand, and wrist strength.

- Mark finger positions on softballs with contact paper or washable paint as a guide to finger placement.

SUMMARY OF SPECIAL OLYMPICS SOFTBALL THROW RULES

- A 12 inch softball is used.

- Any type of throw may be used.

- Throws may be made from a standing position or after a short run within a six foot restraining area.

- The best of three throws is recorded in competition.

- Measurement is from spot ball lands to inside edge of front restraining line.

- Fouls occur when competitors step over restraining or foul line; fouls are not measured but count as trials.

Preparation for Throw

Descriptions are for right handed throwers—reverse for left handers.

Fundamentals

Stand near back restraining line facing direction of throw; space feet comfortably apart—some youngsters stand with feet together, others place them various distances apart.

Get an effective throwing grip; hold ball in one or two hands depending upon which is more natural and comfortable—youngsters with small hands may have to support ball in front of body with nonthrowing hand.

Take an average step forward with left foot; take a shorter step with right foot, turning it to the right.

Bend rear knee so as to lower body into a powerful throwing position; rotate hips and pivot (turn) left foot so entire body now faces to the right; continue to bring right arm back into throwing position, with ball behind right ear and bent right elbow leading (in front of) hand.

Bend left elbow and point it at a 45 degree angle to help guide direction of throw; look over a tree, corner of a building, piece of apparatus, or similar object in line of throw to help achieve proper throwing angle.

Teaching Activities

- Develop step pattern described with following progression—

  √ Take side position with feet together—step with left foot and throw.

  √ Take side position with feet spread about shoulder width apart—bring right foot to left foot, step with left foot, and throw.

  √ Take side position with feet together—step with left foot, bring right foot to left foot, step again with left foot, and throw.

  √ Face direction of throw—pivot on both feet to right, step with left foot, and throw.

  √ Face direction of throw—pivot on both feet to right, step with left foot, bring right foot to left foot, step again with left foot, and throw.

Helpful Hint:

- Mark footprints on floor or blacktop area to help youngsters develop step patterns; use different colors for right and left feet with arrows, if necessary, to guide movement from one step to the next.

- Use imitative throwing in which youngster steps and simulates throwing action to develop form, rhythm, flow, and sequence of movements.

- Concentrate on throwing form by stepping and throwing ball easily; emphasize smooth and coordinated action.

- Include games, relays, and other fun activities which emphasize specific aspects of throwing form. Use activities like—

  √ *Hail to the chief*—divide youngsters into groups of four with *Chief* in front; salute chief, then step and *throw* salute to him; salute with beanbag, fluff ball, or other type of ball then throw *this salute* to chief who catches it and returns to another youngster; continue pattern and give everyone a chance to be chief.

  √ *Partner throw*—play catch with a partner—emphasize specific aspects of throwing form; use beanbag, fluff ball, or other type of ball; increase distance as throwing ability improves.

Throw and Release

Descriptions are for right handed throwers—reverse for left handers.

Fundamentals

Step straight ahead with left foot—keep right hip back and low and right arm bent with ball still behind ear and elbow leading.

Start throwing motion by pushing hard with right foot against ground; straighten right knee and rotate hips as throwing action moves upward and forward across hips to straight left leg; keep head and chest up, in line with direction of throw, and eyes focused on target; keep ball behind right ear and elbow leading.

Use left arm as power whip—move it vigorously to rear to increase speed of right arm as it begins the last phase of the throwing action; develop a throw in which body leads and arm trails.

Extend right arm fully forward; complete release by snapping wrist—release ball at 45 degree angle.

Follow through by bringing hand completely down and right foot forward to front restraining line.

Teaching Activities

Under no circumstances—practice or competition—should a youngster throw hard or far before he has warmed up thoroughly.

- Use imitative throwing in which youngster steps and simulates throwing action to develop form, rhythm, flow, and sequence of throwing movements.

- Throw, emphasizing form—stress one aspect of form at a time; work on it for a few minutes or certain number of throws and then change to another aspect of form. Include a sufficient number of form throws at increasing distances in preparation for all out throws in practice or competition.

- Practice throwing over objects placed at different distances from restraining line to get proper release angle and throwing arc; use football goal posts, improvised targets made from bamboo poles, wooden dowels, broom sticks, and string, or adapt other devices to practice releasing ball at 45 degree angle.

- Devise special exercises and activities for specific aspects of throwing action. For example, take basic position just prior to start of throwing motion with right leg bent and right hip back and low—straighten right knee forcibly, rotate hips, and simulate twisting action of hips which is vital in throwing. Use other activities which emphasize these hip movements—swing a baseball bat, tennis or badminton racquet, throw a discus, or put a shot.

- Include games, relays, and other fun activities which emphasize specific aspects of throwing form. Use activities like—

    √ *Hail to the chief* (p. 91).

    √ *Partner throw* (p. 91).

    √ *Distance relay*—divide youngsters into groups of two, three, or four with each group at opposite ends of a marked throwing area —distance between groups is determined by ability of youngsters. First youngster in one group throws as far as possible—other team lets ball hit ground, retrieves it, and its first man throws ball from point where it struck ground. Continue this pattern until everyone has thrown once (twice, three, five, ten times)—winner is determined by where ball lands on last throw—if in front of line of team that made first throw, it is the winner; if behind this line, opponents win. This can be scored on an individual basis—a member of each team throws and a point is scored after each set of throws; team score is based on cumulative points. This can be an individual activity in which one youngster continuously throws against another.

    NOTE: Throughout these activities emphasize throw, release, and follow through.

Helpful Hints:

- Emphasize form, rhythm, flow, and sequence of movements—the key to good performance is maximum controlled speed, so *gradually* increase speed.

- Have youngsters who tend to foul concentrate on bringing right foot to but not over restraining line on follow through; some may have to shorten length of steps so that follow through does not cause them to go over restraining line. If necessary, begin with lines more than six feet apart so youngsters get used to throwing within a confined area; gradually reduce distance to regulation six feet.

Competitive Preparation

Under no circumstances—practice or competition—should a youngster throw hard or far before he has warmed up thoroughly—include a sufficient number of form throws at increasing distances in preparation for all out throws in practice or competition.

Helpful Hint:

- Mark throwing area with arcs at five foot intervals to make measuring, noting distances, and improvement easier. *Caution:* Understand that when practice is conducted in a marked area, youngsters tend to emphasize distance rather than form.

- Set up throwing area with several sets of six foot restraining lines; divide youngsters into groups of two with one from each group at each end of throwing area; give each group three softballs. First youngster makes three throws; his partner retrieves, and after final throw takes his throws. Continue this pattern for designated time or number of throws. *Caution:* Be sure sufficient distance is allowed between each throwing area.

- Make an all out throw—take three (5, 10, 15, 20, 30) additional throws and see how many surpass initial effort.

- Determine when each youngster obtains his best throw. The number of throws in competition does not permit most throwers to achieve their best performances—they must work up to best throws through all out practice throws; determine this as follows:

    √ Take 20 - 25 all out throws.

    √ Record, chart, or graph each throw in terms of actual distance or how much each throw increases or decreases compared with first effort—note pattern and when best throw occurs.

    √ Repeat this procedure several times—*never more than once a week*—until pattern is established whereby best throw occurs within one or two throws.

    √ Plan premeet practice so best throw occurs on *second* of three competitive throws. For example, if a youngster's best throw occurs on his 16th effort, he should take 14 all out practice throws before his first competitive throw; in this way his 16th all out effort is his second in competition.

- Develop premeet warm-up pattern that includes easy running, some bending and stretching, special arm and shoulder exercises (beware of push-ups, pull-ups and similar strengthening-endurance activities on meet days), some easy throwing, and the needed number of *all out* practice throws.

- Compete against other members of the squad or class or in practice meets against other teams or schools; make intrasquad or practice meets as similar to actual competition as possible.

PENTATHLON

The Special Olympics pentathlon is a test of endurance, speed, agility, and overall athletic ability. It consists of standing long jump, 50 yard dash, softball throw, high jump, and 300 yard run held in the order listed. Pentathlon competition is separate from competition in the individual track and field events. Participation is limited to boys and girls 13 and over, who may not take part in any other Special Olympics events.

Many youngsters who perform at *champ* and *super champ* levels should be considered for the pentathlon. However, don't overlook gutty, highly competitive youngsters who may have the special skills needed for success in the pentathlon even though their fitness and conditioning levels are not at champ or super champ levels. The pentathlon is a tremendous challenge since each youngster competes in every individual event except the mile and therefore must develop the speed, power, endurance, coordination, and skills needed to succeed in these activities.

Since youngsters are preparing to compete in five events, there is little chance for specialization. Practice daily, using drills, warm-ups, fundamentals, and activities described under individual events—standing long jump, pp. 82-84; 50 yard dash, pp. 65-74; softball throw, pp. 89-93; high jump, pp. 84-89; 300 yard run, pp. 65-74. Some general guidelines—

- Work on one track and one field event each day; emphasize aspects of each event in which youngster is weak—form, endurance, speed, start, finish, approach.

- Do not practice standing long jump and high jump on same day except during time trials, intrasquad competition, or practice meets when youngsters compete in all events.

- Pick one day, preferably Friday, for time trials, intrasquad competition, or practice meets in all five events. This helps develop the kind of endurance needed to compete in the pentathlon.

- Emphasize weak events by having youngsters perform all five events as in competition and then spend rest of day's practice time equally on two weakest events.

- Use following chart for guidance in determining a youngster's comparative ability in each event.

Pentathlon Scoring

Youngsters receive points in each event based on the order in which they finish; all events carry the same point value with respect to total pentathlon score. For example, if there are 30 competitors and a youngster finishes first in all five events, he scores 150 points—5 x 30; a youngster finishing

last in all events scores five points—5 x 1. The youngster with the highest number of points for the five events wins.

With this scoring system it is logical to concentrate on a youngster's weakest events, emphasize fair events, and maintain performance levels in strong events—don't let him slip. The reason for this approach is simple—the more a youngster improves weak events, the better his chances of improving his relative position in competition.

Another consideration is the youngster's potential for improvement in each event. For example, a youngster who has run a great deal but jumped very little will usually improve more in jumping events than in running activities. Similarly, the characteristics of the 300 yard run and softball throw are such that more rapid and greater improvement can be realized than in the other three events. Further, events like the high jump, standing long jump, and 50 yard dash are subject to performance plateaus or leveling off. Planning pentathlon practice sessions is a complicated and complex procedure in which each competitor's performance patterns, experience, and abilities must be considered. The following chart is included simply as a guide and aid in developing and organizing a one week pentathlon practice routine.

The pentathlon is a demanding event—five activities in one day. It is not easy to get competitors in condition for competition while making training and practice fun, interesting, exciting, and challenging. Use games, relays, activities, drills, described for individual events and motivational devices discussed in the introduction to the track and field section to stimulate youngsters to peak performances.

SELECTED TRACK AND FIELD REFERENCES

Canham, Don. *Field Techniques Illustrated.* New York: A. S. Barnes and Company, 1952.

Canham, Don (Consultant). *How to Improve Your Track and Field.* Chicago: The Athletic Institute (805 Merchandise Mart), 1956. (Filmstrip with same title complements publication.)

Canham, Don. *Track Techniques Illustrated.* New York: A. S. Barnes and Company, 1952.

Dodd, J. H. *Jumping.* (A Know the Game Book—Coach Yourself Series.) Great Britain: Dixon and Stell Limited (Cross Hills near Keighley, Yorkshire), 1962.

Luke, Brother G. *Coaching High School Track and Field.* Englewood Cliffs, New Jersey: Prentice-Hall, Inc., 1958.

Winter, Lloyd. *So You Want To Be A High Jumper.* San Francisco, California: Fearon Publishers, 1958.

Winter, Lloyd. *So You Want To Be A Sprinter.* San Francisco, California: Fearon Publishers, 1956.

PENTATHLON EVENT EVALUATION CHART

		50 Yard Dash		300 Yard Run		Standing Long Jump		Softball Throw		High Jump	
		13 to 15 Years	16 Years Up	13 to 15 Years	16 Years Up	13 to 15 Years	16 Years Up	13 to 15 Years	16 Years Up	13 to 15 Years	16 Years Up
Boys Good		5.8 sec.	5.9 sec.	43 sec.	40 sec.	8'2"	8'5"	229'	250'	4'11"	5'2"
Fair		7.1 sec.	6.1 sec.	56 sec.	49 sec.	6'4"	7'5"	181'	204'	4'5"	4'10"
Weak		7.4 sec.	6.3 sec.	60 sec.	51 sec.	5'11"	7'2"	142'	176'	4'0"	4'6"
Girls Good		6.4 sec.	6.2 sec.	54 sec.	43 sec.	7'2"	8'2"	131'	137'	3'11"	4'2"
Fair		7.8 sec.	7.9 sec.	66 sec.	70 sec.	5'6"	5'8"	95'	98'	3'5"	3'10"
Weak		8.0 sec.	8.2 sec.	72 sec.	73 sec.	5'1"	5'3"	86'	81'	3'0"	3'6"

This chart gives an indication of a youngster's comparative ability in each pentathlon event. Use this as a guide in planning practice sessions so that participants emphasize weak events, strengthen fair events, and retain performance levels in good events. While there are three competitive age categories—13 to 15, 16 to 18, and 19 and over—only two age breakdowns are provided; use *16 years up* for both older groups.

SUMMARY OF SPECIAL OLYMPICS PENTATHLON RULES

- Competitors must be 13 or over to participate in the pentathlon.

- Pentathlon participants may not enter any other Special Olympics events.

- Events are conducted in the following order— standing long jump, 50 yard dash, softball throw, high jump, and 300 yard run. Participants compete against each other in separate pentathlon heats, sections, or events, and not against those taking part in individual Special Olympics events.

- All events are weighted equally and a competitor's score is based on how he ranks in each event. For example, with 10 participants, the winner of each pentathlon event receives 10 points, the last or tenth place finisher earns one point, with the rest earning between two and nine points depending on where they finish. If two youngsters tie for a position, points are split; with ten participants, each of two tied for first receives 9½ points; each of three 9 points. A competitor's total score is the sum of points earned in all five events.

	Monday	Tuesday	Wednesday	Thursday	Friday
Warm-up	All pentathlon participants warm-up with rest of squad, group, or class. Individuals not part of group programs follow warm-up procedures and routines outlined in track and field practice cycles, pp. 45-63.				
Special Exercises and Drills	All pentathlon participants do *Flexible Five* and other special drills and activities outlined in trace and field practice cycles, pp. 45-63. Stay with rest of squad, group, or class for these exercises and drills. Remainder of practice routine for pentathlon participants emphasizes pentathlon events.				
Track Event	10 min.—30 yd. wind sprints (p. 71). 10 min.—100 yd. speed repeats (p. 69). 5 min.—finishing drills (p. 73).	Run one pyramid (p. 71). Use remaining time to run on hill (p. 69), work on form (p. 69), or tire pull (p. 69).	Practice starts as follows — 10 min.—form starts (p. 72) 6 to 8 reaction starts (p. 72); use 300 yd. run starting area Run four all out 110's with maximum 1 min. rest interval	Special emphasis on sprint form as follows—5 min.— run tall (p. 69); 5 min.—form running (p. 69); 5 min.—exercises and arm accelerator (p. 69). 10 min.—divide between neutral-man-neutral (p. 71) and shift gears (p. 71).	Participate in practice pentathlon—go through all five events exactly as in competition. After completing all five events, divide remaining practice time between two weakest events *Note:* Do not practice complete pentathlon before end of fourth or fifth week of special training.
Field Event	High Jump	Softball Throw	High Jump	Standing Long Jump	
	10 min.—check high jump steps (p. 86). 10 min.—form jumping 6 in. under best height (p. 86).	10 min.—form throwing; emphasizing rhythm, flow, and sequence of movements (pp. 90-92). Take as many all out throws as possible in 10 min.— chart increase or decrease of each throw in comparison with first throw (p. 93).	Divide time between drills emphasizing lead leg (p. 86), and trail leg (p. 87).	Divide time equally —spend 5 min. on preliminary drills (p. 83), 5 on take off drills (p. 83), 5 on in air drills (p. 83), and 5 on landing drills (p. 83).	
Warm Down and Fun Activities	All pentathlon participants complete practice sessions with rest of squad, group, or class. Individuals not part of group program complete practice sessions with some type of easy running, jogging, walking, and/or slow/rhythmical bending/stretching/flexibility activities, and/or some type of individual fun activities.				

Volleyball

Ten lesson cycles have been designed to help you coach a successful Special Olympics volleyball team. A youngster must develop three fundamentals to enjoy volleyball and to achieve a certain amount of personal success.

- Hit or bat the ball
- Serve the ball
- Know when and how to rotate

These skills and concepts must be developed and reinforced for individuals and teams to be successful in Special Olympics volleyball. For purposes of these lesson cycles —

- *Bat* or *hit* mean to strike the ball.
- *Pass* means to bat or hit the ball to a teammate.
- *Volley* means to hit or bat the ball two or more times which may or may not include one or more passes and a hit over the net.
- *Net* means net or net substitutes, such as rope, string, or rags hung between trees or high jump standards. With youngsters use the word *net* only when referring to an actual net.

Lesson cycles have been developed to provide individual, partner, small and large group, and team activities. These cycles contain all information needed to teach individual and team skills from basic fundamentals through advanced play for Special Olympics competition. Cycles provide realistic progressions and variations in hitting, passing, volleying, and serving. Basic techniques are introduced and more difficult activities suggested to help talented youngsters learn skills they can use in volleyball. For example, youngsters can learn to put *English* or a curve on the serve by using a variety of wrist and elbow movements and by hitting the ball above, below, left, or right of center. They can increase accuracy in passing or serving by aiming at targets of various sizes and shapes on the floor or wall. As youngsters develop greater skill, reduce the size of the targets and/or put tires, contact paper, masking tape, hoops, or similar items on the floor to restrict movement. When working on individual skills, be sure to provide each youngster with a ball or balloon— interest is kept high and disciplinary problems low when each child is doing something he likes. Demonstrate and let children play and move as much as possible — keep talk and explanations to a minimum. Make this an action program in which kids learn by doing.

Suggest volleyball fun activities for home practice that promote family or ward group togetherness. Invite parents and ward attendants to one or two meetings where volleyball activities they can encourage and lead are discussed and demonstrated. Provide opportunities for parents to practice, to learn skills, and to play the game.

How an individual coach uses these lesson cycles will vary according to the ability of the youngsters, number of participants, number of volunteer helpers, length and frequency of practice sessions. In first practice session find out where each youngster is in terms of learned or natural volleyball skills and proceed from there. Some youngsters will be able to bypass familiarization and exploration activities emphasized in Cycles 1 and 2. Others may need much work on these activities even before moving to beginning and intermediate volleyball skills. Some youngsters will be able to start using a regulation volleyball immediately while others will need to practice patiently and diligently with balloons, beach balls, plastic balls, rubber balls, or partially deflated volleyballs before using a regulation ball. Be flexible and aware of individual needs as you use the cycles. How long you spend on each cycle depends on your individual situation.

While mentally retarded boys and girls have learned such advanced skills as the dig pass, blocking at the net, and playing the ball off the net, these skills have not been included in the cycles so more time can be spent on beginning and intermediate individual and team skills. Spiking and the overhand serve are not included because Special Olympics rules prohibit their use.

Reminder

Before starting *skill building* activities in each session be sure to spend a minimum of ten minutes on conditioning and fitness activities (pp. 6-40).

CYCLE 1
(Howdy Doody Mr. Ball)

BALL FAMILIARIZATION ACTIVITIES

Helpful Hint:

- As youngsters perform various skills, movements, and patterns, note performance levels of each. For example, some youngsters may use volleyballs adequately for some activities but may have to use partially deflated volleyballs, rubber playground balls, plastic balls, beach balls, or balloons for other activities such as batting or hitting.

- *Move ball* around various parts of the body—neck, head, chest, waist, thighs, knees, ankles, feet, arms, hands, legs.

- *Move ball* around parts of the body of a partner.

- *Balance ball* on various parts of the body—head, shoulder, hand, back of hand, arm, foot.

- *Toss ball* from hand-to-hand; to various heights; with two hands and catch it in one hand; with one hand and catch it in same (opposite) hand; clap hands (once, twice, many times) before catching ball; turn around before catching ball; catch ball near floor (ankles, knees, waist, chest, head); let ball bounce once (any number of times) before catching it; in various ways to a partner.

- *Bounce ball* with two hands to various heights and catch—use two hands, one hand, other hand, left (right) hand to bounce ball and perform movements from listing above; bounce ball continuously with both hands (one hand, other hand); bounce ball to a partner; bounce ball so it bounces twice before reaching partner.

- *Toss ball* against a wall, let it bounce, and catch it with two hands (one hand, other hand); bounce ball off the floor, hit the wall, and catch it on fly; toss ball off wall and catch it; substitute a partner for wall.

- *Roll ball* at specific targets on a wall; stand close to the wall, roll the ball, and then bat it back and forth (still rolling) with both hands; roll ball back and forth with a partner.

- *Stand close* to wall and pass ball back and forth at target like basketball chest pass; add variations by changing distance from (size, shape, position of) target; bat ball over a line drawn at various heights on the wall.

- *Hit ball* with palms of hands, thumbs together, when it is tossed.

- *Hit ball* into air with open palm (closed fist, end of closed fist). Devise other activities and approaches for youngsters to use individually, with partners, and in small groups to explore and experiment in handling a ball so as to become more familiar with it. Encourage each child to discover his own ways of handling, hitting, rolling, tossing, and bouncing a ball—make and keep it *fun*.

Helpful Hint:

- When working with youngsters who have difficulty in communicating verbally, devise your own approaches to overcome this problem. For example, use a tetherball with its attached rope or attach a whiffle or other kind of ball to a string to encourage a youngster to hit the ball. Dangle the ball in front of a child so he must reach to hit it. Move the ball slowly past him so he must hit a moving target; have him kick the ball, hit it with his knee, head, or other parts of the body. Start with the child sitting on the floor and then follow the same procedure while he kneels, sits in a chair, and finally stands. With many of these youngsters simply holding or moving the ball near them results in action; others will follow the leader or another child.

CYCLE 2
(And What Can You Do With A Ball?)

BALL EXPLORATION

Helpful Hint:

- Use volleyball, partially deflated volleyball. rubber playground ball, plastic ball, beach ball, or balloon as appropriate for each youngster.

Continue on an exploratory basis many ball familiarization activities introduced in Cycle 1—give youngsters opportunities to experiment and explore through solving movement problems involving balls. Ask such questions as:

- What can you do with a ball?

- Can you roll the ball, run around it, and catch it?

- How high can you toss the ball? Can you toss the ball high and catch it low?

- How high can you hit the ball?

- How many times can you bounce the ball without missing?

- Can you bounce it with one hand? In a tire?

- Can you stand in a tire (on a balance beam) and bounce the ball?

- Can you toss the ball off the wall and catch it?

- Can you bat the ball against the wall two (three, five, 50) times?
- Can you bounce the ball over a line? To a partner?
- Can you toss the ball back and forth with a partner?
- Can you bat the ball back and forth with a partner?
- Can you bounce the ball on the floor to a partner and have him catch it? Can you make it bounce twice before he catches it?
- Can you bat the ball off the floor to your partner after he bounces it to you?

Devise your own questions and problems according to deficiencies and strengths youngsters show in performing skills, patterns, and movements.

CYCLE 3
(Up-Up-Up-And Over)

Helpful Hint

- For each youngster, it is of utmost importance that you select and use the appropriate ball—volleyball, partially deflated volleyball, rubber playground ball, plastic ball, beach ball, balloon.

Over the Net

Partners volley ball back and forth over the net to each other. Provide individual challenges for each pair such as:

- Can you hit the ball back and forth over the net with your partner?
- How many times can you and your partner hit the ball without missing?
- Can you hit the ball high over the net?
- Can you hit the ball so it just gets over the net?
- Can you hit the ball to your partner so he can hit it without moving his feet?
- Can you hit the ball so your partner has to move to his right (left) to reach and hit it?

Self Volley

Give each youngster a ball—have him keep it in the air as long as he can. To add interest see who can hit the ball the longest period of time or make the greatest number of consecutive hits without missing.

Line Volley

Divide into groups of four or five with one youngster eight feet or more in front of the others who are in a straight line about four feet apart. Player in front (point man) hits ball to end man

Garbage Man

Divide group into two equal teams; place one team on each side of a net or net substitute. Use beanbags and balls of all sizes—on signal all throw beanbags and balls over the net into other team's court. As balls come into a team's court, players recover and throw them back—try to keep own side as clean and clear of balls as possible. Team with fewest balls on its sides after stipulated time wins.

Helpful Hint

- Continue, expand, or review ball handling activities from Cycle 1 at appropriate times during Cycle 2.

who returns it to point man who hits to the next man, continuing in this way until the ball reaches the player at the far end or returns to the first player in line; change point man and continue until all have had a chance in front. In some instances, the coach may have to start as point man in which case the activity can be called *Coach's Ball.*

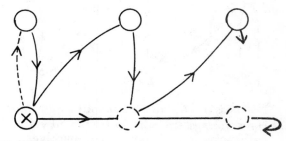

Wall Volley

Draw a line on the wall at net height or lower if necessary. Give each youngster a ball and have him volley the ball against the wall as in self volley above. Gradually increase distance the youngster stands from the wall and the height of the line as skill and confidence increase.

Circle Volley

Divide into groups of four or five with each forming a circle. Have youngsters keep the ball in the air by volleying back and forth. To add interest have competition between groups to see which one can keep the ball in the air the longest without missing. Have youngsters count the number of hits they make or time them.

Variations:

Place one or more youngsters in middle of a circle; give each of these youngsters a ball; pass ball from middleman to player on circle in front of him; pass ball back to middleman who passes it to next youngster on circle; continue to alternate from middleman to next player on circle as middlemen turn (pivot) use as many balls as middlemen.

Middleman passes ball to players on circle with no prescribed order.

Up and Over

Divide squad into two teams and place young-sters in random formation on opposite sides of net—have them play with an unlimited number of hits. Let players toss ball over net as a substitute for the serve or coach may serve.

Helpful Hint

- Use ball familiarization activities from Cycle 1 and exploration activities from Cycle 2 between individual, partner, and small group activities in Cycle 3.

CYCLE 4
(It Don't Mean A Thing If You Can't Serve With Zing)

Zig Zag Volley

Divide youngsters into groups of six with pairs facing each other in lines eight to ten feet apart or closer if necessary. Players hit the ball in zig zag fashion as shown in the diagram. When the ball reaches the end of the line, start it back in the same zig zag pattern. Use more than one ball to keep youngsters alert, to speed up action, and to create enthusiasm.

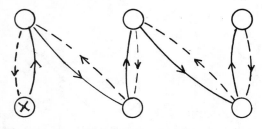

If necessary, break zig zag volley into steps:
- Have youngsters work in pairs and volley the ball back and forth between themselves.
- Add a third player and have the three volley the ball around the triangle.
- Have one of the three players hit the ball to another who returns it to him; he hits to the third youngster who returns it to the first; the pattern continues in this manner.
- Combine two groups of three together to introduce the zig zag volley.
- Add one player at a time to a group of three until all six are included if the increase from three to six is too great for youngsters.
- Include more than six youngsters especially when using more than one ball.
- Have youngsters hit to players on the other line in no set pattern using one or more balls.

Exploratory Serve

Ask youngsters how many different ways they can hit the ball over the net. Ask specifically if they can hold the ball in one hand and hit it with the other hand. If necessary, direct youngster to an appropriate position (procedure is for right handers—reverse for left handers).

- Stand with the left foot forward and hold the ball belt high in the left hand with elbow straight.
- Step with the left foot and at the same time hit the ball off your hand—follow through to the net.

Other questions can be phrased as follows:
- Can you hit the ball high over the net? Still higher?
- Can you hit the ball so that it lands way back in other court? Still further back?
- Can you hit the ball so that it lands near a designated object or target? Close to the net?
- What happens if you hit the ball with an open palm? A closed fist? A partially closed fist? End of closed fist?
- Can you hit three (five, ten) balls in a row over the net without missing.
- How many balls can you hit over the net in 10 (20, 30) seconds?

Garbage Man Serve

Play the same as garbage man (see Cycle 2) except that players must serve rather than throw balls across the net.

Do youngsters still need—
- Ball Familiarization Activities (Cycle 1)?
- Exploratory Activities (Cycle 2)?

Will they benefit from more—

Self Volley (Cycle 3)?

Line Volley (Cycle 3)?

Wall Volley (Cycle 3)?

Circle Volley (Cycle 3)?

Over the Net (Cycle 3)?

Up and Over (Cycle 3)?

CYCLE 5
(Be Good — Be Better — Be Best)

Circle Volley (Cycle 3)

Circle Serve

One youngster gets in the middle of a circle. Have him serve the ball to a player on the circle who catches and serves the ball back. Continue until the middleman has served to everyone in the group; rotate so that every youngster has a turn in the middle. Include same variations and adaptations as outlined for circle volley (Cycle 3).

Team Formation

Introduce team formation according to the rules under which the team will play. Play *up and over* (Cycle 3) with player in serving position serving the ball; continue to play with unlimited hits. Give each youngster a chance to serve by having server and teammates exchange positions. Introduce concepts that only the serving team can score and that an individual and team continue to serve until they lose the volley or play.

Helpful Hint:

- Have each net man start about an arm's length from the net so that he can turn and face the back lines when the ball is hit deep and pivot to face the other side of the net as he or a teammate hits the ball.

Wall or Door Volley

Give each youngster a ball and have him volley it against the wall (Cycle 3) or over a door.

Wall or Door Serve

Give each youngster a ball and have him serve it against the wall or over a door.

Wall or Door Serve and Volley

Give each youngster a ball and have him serve and then volley three (five, ten) times against the wall or over a door.

Review
Individual skills alone:

Self Volley (Cycle 3)

Wall Volley (Cycle 3)

Individual skills with a partner
or in small groups:

Over the Net (Cycle 3)

Line Volley (Cycle 3)

Circle Volley (Cycle 3)

Zig Zag Volley (Cycle 4)

Individual skills in team activities:

Up and Over (Cycle 3)

Garbage Man Serve (Cycle 4)

CYCLE 6
(Again And Again And Again)

Up and Over

Play *up and over* as in Cycle 5. Introduce the concept of rotation and practice it in fun ways such as rotate on signal, to music, as a maze with lines to follow, as a part of original games. Play *up and over* using proper rotation.

Three and Over Volleyball

Require youngsters to volley the ball three times on their side of the net before hitting it over the net. This develops team play and the idea of moving the ball to the best possible position before hitting it over the net. Have players count hits— one! two! three! over!

Rotation Practice

Practice rotation as in *up and over.*

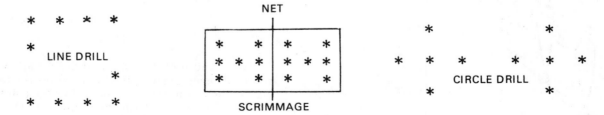

Have youngsters not actually scrimmaging at any one time work on individual, partner, or small group activities.

Special Olympics Volleyball Scrimmage

Divide youngsters into regulation Special Olympics volleyball teams for scrimmage or practice games. During these games look for strengths and weaknesses of individual players and for combinations of players who work especially well together. Use scrimmages as a basis for individual, partner, group, and team activities in future practice sessions. Encourage youngsters to work at home on skills in which they need extra practice.

Keep all youngsters active during scrimmage sessions. Facilities will determine how you do this.

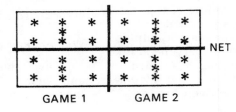

SMALL GROUP ACTIVITIES

INDIVIDUAL ACTIVITIES

NET

GAME 1   GAME 2

Arrange court so that two or more scrimmages are in progress.

Be sure that all youngsters take part in every scrimmage.

May a day never end without a plan for tomorrow.

Individual Practice

Have youngsters practice individual skills in which they need the most work. Include such activities as self volley, wall volley, partner volley, over the net, wall or door serve, partner serve.

Extra time spent on serving is a wise investment—

Exploratory Serve (Cycle 4)

Garbage Man Serve (Cycle 4)

Circle Serve (Cycle 5)

Wall/Door Serve (Cycle 5)

CYCLE 7
(Putting It All Together)

Shuttle Serve

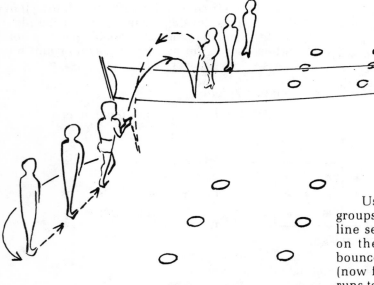

Use a shuttle formation and divide squad into groups of three to five players. First player in one line serves to the first player in the opposite line on the other side of the net who lets the ball bounce, picks it up and serves to the second player (now first) in other line. After a player serves he runs to the back of the opposite (same) line.

Accuracy Serve

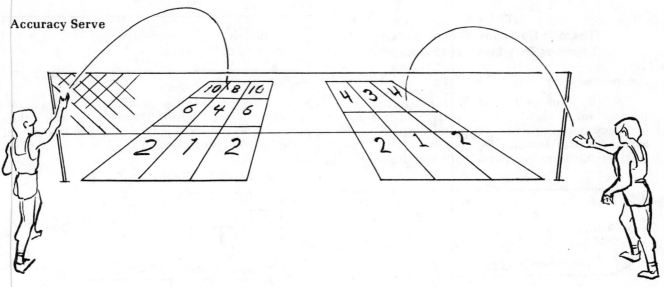

Divide the court into areas and ask youngsters to serve the ball into designated areas to improve serving accuracy.

Variations:

Place various size objects such as bicycle tires, automobile tires, boxes, waste baskets, hoops, floor targets, contact paper shapes at different places on the court.

Place a rope three (two, one) feet above the net so that the serve must go over the net and under the rope. Combine this with other accuracy serve approaches.

Underhand Hit

Divide youngsters into groups of two. One partner tosses the ball and the other hits it. The tosser throws the ball low—below the waist—so that his partner must hit it in an underhand motion. Alternate so that each youngster has a chance to practice the underhand hit.

Three and Over Volleyball (Cycle 6)

Individual Skills

Overhand hitting—underhand hitting—serving (by yourself, with partners, in small groups, as a team).

Special Olympics Volleyball Scrimmage (Cycle 6)

The only difference between CHAMP and CHUMP IS U! PRACTICE! COACH! MOTIVATE! REVIEW!

Team Skills

Rotating—working together.

103

CYCLE 8
(There Is No Team Without Work, Together They Mean Teamwork)

> *A difference is a difference only if it makes a difference.*

Around the Horn

Set up four or five stations for self volley, partner volley, wall volley, wall or door serve, accuracy serve. Divide youngsters equally and assign them to stations. In most cases all youngsters at each station participate simultaneously.

Have them practice designated skill at each station for indicated length of time after which they move from station to station in predetermined order. Have youngsters move on whistle or other signal.

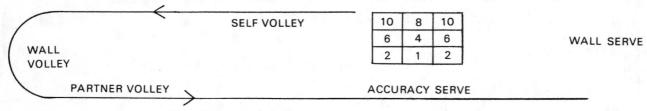

Note: Set up more than one station for each activity.

Teamwork

Divide squad into teams as for scrimmage. Have one player on front line toss the ball to a teammate on the back line; this player hits ball to a teammate on the middle line who in turn hits it to a teammate on the front line who in turn sets it up for a front line teammate who hits the ball over the net. Players rotate so all have a chance to practice in all positions.

Helpful Hint:
- Have back or middle line players loft ball with a soft easy to handle pass two to three feet higher than net so net man can place the ball where he wants it to go.

Three and Over Volleyball (Cycle 6)

Special Olympics Volleyball Scrimmage (Cycle 6)

Emphasize using all hits and moving the ball into good position.

Keep the FUN in FUNDAMENTALS with a volleyball field day:
- Self volley
- Wall volley
- Partner volley
- Line volley
- Circle volley
- Zig zag volley
- Accuracy serve
- Add your own events
- Have players devise events
- Develop a fun scoring system

CYCLE 9
(We've Come A Long Way Together Baby)

Teamwork (Cycle 8)

Exploratory Serving

Line players up on both back lines of the court for *accuracy serve* (Cycle 7). After a few minutes, ask what happens —
- If the wrist is twisted or turned as the hand or fist contacts the ball?
- If the hand is pulled back as it contacts the ball?
- If the ball is hit above (below) the middle?
- If the ball is hit left (right) of the middle?

- If the ball is hit above (below) *and* left (right) of the middle?
- If the ball is contacted with the knuckles?
- If the ball is hit with the back of the hand?
- If the ball is hit on the wrist?

Use your observations as a basis for providing each youngster with additional ways to serve.

Helpful Hints:
- Players can learn to put *English* or a curve on either an open palm or fist serve to make it break, float, spin, dip, and difficult to return. These advanced techniques should not be introduced until a player can consistently control serves without spin.
- To apply spin for a ball that breaks to the left, simply hit the ball below its center and to the

right side with a twisting motion of fingers, wrist, and elbow. Reverse spin for a ball that breaks to the right is applied by twisting wrist and elbow so that contact is on the left side of the ball. By quickly pulling the hand and arm back as contact is made, the ball will float and act like a knuckle ball in baseball.

Shuttle Serve (Cycle 7)

Special Olympics Volleyball Scrimmage (Cycle 6)

Around the Horn (Cycle 8)

Now is the time to polish and refine all that has gone behind.

CYCLE 10
(Rivalry And Competition Stimulate A Youth's Ambition)

Pregame Procedures

Provide youngsters with opportunities to prepare for game competition and tournament play. Use warm-up activities that include all skills required in actual play:

> *Individual ball handling*—self volley, wall volley
>
> *Partner and/or small group ball handling*—partner volley, line volley, circle volley, zig zag volley
>
> *Serving*—shuttle serve, accuracy serve
>
> *Team play*—teamwork, three and over

Team Tournament

Divide youngsters into competitive teams. If necessary, divide playing area into courts that are smaller than regulation size so that all teams can play at the same time. If this is not possible, while two teams play, others should continue warm-up activities and other drills to sharpen skills. Ways to set up four or six team tournaments are shown below. Use the six-team approach with five teams —each team practices or works on various drills when not involved in competition. By limiting each game to a given number of minutes, a tournament can be completed in one practice session. Tournament play can continue from day-to-day with one or more rounds scheduled over the course of several days.

> NOTE: Team 1 always plays on the same court—all other teams rotate one court clockwise for each succeeding round.

A winner never quits; a quitter never wins.

Six Team Tournament

Net	1	2	3
	6	5	4

Round		Round	
1	1 vs 6	4	1 vs 4
	2 vs 5		5 vs 3
	3 vs 4		6 vs 2
2	1 vs 2	5	1 vs 5
	3 vs 6		6 vs 4
	4 vs 5		2 vs 3
3	1 vs 3		
	4 vs 2		
	5 vs 6		

Four Team Tournament

Net	1	2
	4	3

Round	
1	1 vs 4
	2 vs 3
2	1 vs 3
	4 vs 2
3	1 vs 2
	3 vs 4

Volleyball Fundamentals

Two Hand Overhand Pass

The two hand overhand pass is the fundamental and preferred volleyball pass.

Take forward stride position with either leg forward, knees bent and body crouched slightly.

Hold hands high, palms forward, fingers spread, tilted back, and slightly curved.

Keep elbows away from body.

Look up at the ball through the window formed by the thumbs and first fingers; move the window right or left but continue to look up at the ball through this window.

Contact ball with fleshy part of fingers—not palms.

Contact ball above shoulder level.

Straighten elbows and knees at time of contact.

Hit ball sharply upward with vigorous use of fingers.

Follow ball upward with eyes, hands, and body as wrists flick or snap forward.

Stress the importance of keeping eyes on the ball at all times; when a ball is high, raise hands above head and look under hands; when a ball is lower, look over hands.

Pass ball forward to a teammate or to a designated spot along the net in front of a net man or hit it over the net.

Use two hands whenever possible—one hand is a last resort.

Drop down to hit low balls with overhand motion whenever possible—underhand is less effective.

Coaching Tips

Problem	Possible Solution	Problem	Possible Solution
• Contact with palms.	• Keep fingers widely spread; curl fingers slightly forward; develop greater finger strength. Keep elbows away from body; continue to look through the window.	• Hit into net.	• Assume crouch position with fingers tilted and palms facing upward; drop to knees when hitting; extend arms and body upward when contacting ball; exaggerate height; follow through to ceiling.

Open Palm Serve

The *open palm serve* is the basic serve. (Directions for right handers—reverse for left handers.)

Take position with front of body facing net; bend from waist slightly.

Place feet in stride position with left foot forward—make sure both feet remain in serving circle until after contact is made.

Hold ball in left hand about waist high, in front of and slightly to the right and clear of the body.

Take a step with left foot to start serve, obtain momentum, and gain power.

Use a pendulum motion; elbow straight and wrist firm.

Coordinate or time body swing and arm movement so they are simultaneous.

Keep eye on back of ball.

Strike ball at base of palm with hand open and fingers cupped slightly.

Follow through naturally and completely—reach forward with right hand and arm in direction ball is to go, straightening knees and extending body.

Coaching Tips

Problem	Possible Solution	Problem	Possible Solution
• Insufficient force.	• Hit ball harder; increase body movement; emphasize initial step; follow through completely—reach for ceiling; exaggerate height, depth, and distance.	• Poor direction.	• Follow through in direction ball is to go; emphasize initial step; use motivating targets.
		• Insufficient height.	• Contact underside of ball; emphasize follow through—hand to ceiling; exaggerate height—hit ceiling; generate more power.

Fist Serve

The *fist serve* is basically the same as the open palm serve except—

Close hand to make a full fist.

Hit ball with knuckles, heel of hand, or thumb side of fist.

Two Hand Underhand Pass

The *two hand underhand pass* is used when the ball is below a player's waist to get it in a better position for a teammate or as a last resort to hit the ball over the net.

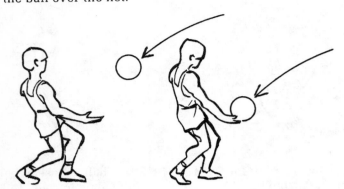 

Place feet a comfortable distance apart with knees slightly bent — rise to meet ball, straightening legs on contact.

Cup hands with palms up, fingers pointed down, and little fingers together.

Hit ball with lifting motion with elbows bent slightly — combine strength of legs and forward thrust of hips to provide power and lift to ball.

Hit ball with control so that it leaves fingers on contact — avoid catching/throwing ball.

Contact ball with fingers — not palms.

Follow through by stepping in direction of hit — swing arms upward to get sufficient height to get ball over the net or to a teammate.

Use two hands whenever possible — one hand is a last resort.

Coaching Tips

Problem	Possible Solution
• Lack of force.	• Get under ball and hit it harder and higher; use legs and hips to obtain power; follow through to ceiling.
• Poor direction.	• Follow through in direction ball is to go; check feet position with respect to direction ball is to go; turn body in direction ball is to go.
• Insufficient height.	• Get under ball; drop to knees when hitting; exaggerate height; emphasize follow through — palms to ceiling.

SUMMARY OF SPECIAL OLYMPICS
VOLLEYBALL RULES

You must know and teach the squad the Special Olympics Volleyball Rules. Emphasize these as individual and team skills are introduced in various cycles.

- No spiking permitted; ball must go over net in a looping manner.
- Ball must be served with an underhand motion from the serving circle in the middle of the court and must go over the net in an arch.
- Ball may not be served more than twice in succession to the same player on receiving team. If this occurs on an otherwise legal serve, ball must be served again.
- First serve must clear the net and land in receiving team's court to avoid loss of serve.
- Ball must be batted; throwing and catching are illegal.
- Players may not reach over net to strike ball nor may they follow through from a striking motion and go over net.
- Ball may be hit three times before going over net—*must go over on fourth hit.*
- Net is a maximum of eight feet high but may be lower by mutual agreement.
- Court may be either 20 by 40 feet or 30 by 60 feet. There are seven players on a team when the smaller court is used and ten when the larger court is used.
- Coeducational volleyball is permitted if individual tournament committees agree. In coeducational competition, three players of a seven-member-team must be girls; five players of a ten-member team must be girls.
- A back line player may not come to the front line to hit the ball over the net.

Helpful Hint:

- Plan regular strategy sessions with the team to be sure players know and understand rules.

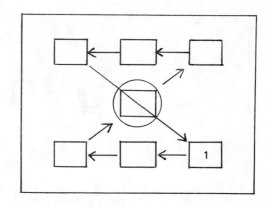

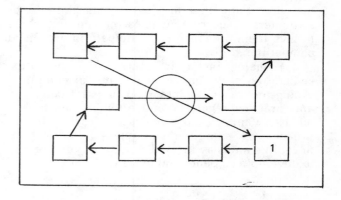

SELECTED VOLLEYBALL REFERENCES

Egstrom, Glen H. and Schaafsma, Frances. *Volleyball.* Dubuque, Iowa: Wm. C. Brown Company Publishers, 1966.

Emery, Curtis Ray. *Modern Volleyball.* New York, New York: The Macmillan Co., 1953.

Laveaga, Robert E. (Consultant). *How to Improve Your Volleyball.* Chicago, Illinois: Athletic Institute (805 Merchandise Mart). (Filmstrip with same title complements publication.)

Laveaga, Robert E. *Volleyball.* New York, New York: A. S. Barnes and Company, 1942.

Odeneal, William T. and Wilson, Harry E. *Beginning Volleyball.* Belmont, California. Wadsworth Publishing Company, Inc., 1962.

Welch, J. Edmund (Editor). *How to Play and Teach Volleyball.* New York, New York: Association Press, 1960.

We can say with some assurance that although children may be the victims of fate, they will not be the victims of our neglect.

John F. Kennedy

Swimming

The Special Olympics swimming program is designed for boys and girls who know how to swim. *It is not intended to teach nonswimmers to swim,*[1] but rather to provide opportunities for swimmers to learn to swim faster and better and to give them a chance to participate in organized competition.

A major factor in successful competitive swimming is a high level of physical condition. Youngsters must get into good physical condition and practice regularly and often. A coach who makes swimming fun and uses a variety of approaches to stimulate youngsters to work hard to get into and stay in good condition is on the way to developing a beneficial program for all.

Practice Cycles

Ten practice cycles contain activities to help condition swimmers and teach them basic fundamentals necessary for success in competitive swimming. Cycles provide necessary information for organizing practice sessions efficiently to meet the individual needs of each swimmer. Cycles are based on practice sessions lasting from 35 to 60 minutes, excluding out-of-pool warm-up. When less time is allocated for practice, adjust cycles so proportionate time is spent on each major component. Regardless of length of practice, make sure each activity listed under stroke work and special fundamentals (Cycles 1-7) and event workouts (Cycles 8-10) is included. This adjustment will be necessary when swimmers require more than suggested rest and relaxation time between action activities.

Cycles are divided into five segments:

- Warm-up — 4 to 8 minutes
- Conditioning — 5 to 10 minutes
- Stroke work — 15 to 20 minutes
- Special fundamentals — 10 to 20 minutes
- Fun activities — 5 to 10 minutes

Warm-down, a method of gradually easing out of a vigorous period of exercise with a slow decrease in the intensity of activity, is as important to safety and condition as proper warm-up; specific attention must be given to warm-down in every practice session. Cycles 1-7 incorporate warm-down in fun activities such as relays, games, and novelty approaches. In Cycles 8-10 warm-down is accomplished through slow, easy, and relaxing swimming or aquatic activity such as floating, gliding, easy bobbing, rhythmic breathing, or form swimming.

Landlubber's Loosen-up is an out-of-pool warm-up stressing loosening up activities including bending and stretching, flexibility, and abdominal endurance. Warm-up time should not take away from actual time in the pool.

Five-Fathoms is an in-pool conditioning program designed to develop and increase endurance, coordination, balance, agility, and flexibility. Basic aquatic activities with variations are provided to encourage youngsters to work hard to increase fitness. In addition to fitness activities described for each practice session, information about nonstop rhythmical aquatic routines (p. 136), interval training (p. 128), and circuit training (p. 130), is included. Encourage swimmers to engage in non-pool conditioning activities after practice and to participate in activities at home, on the ward, or in the cottage to develop general strength, endurance, speed, and power. For additional information on conditioning and fitness, see pp. 6-40.

Stroke work is designed to improve arm action, leg action, breath control, and the total stroke. For purposes of this guide, *crawl* refers to a stroke, and *freestyle* to an event. For each event, an analysis of the components of each stroke is presented in terms of basic fundamentals, teaching progressions, and helpful hints.

Special fundamentals include tactics and strategies necessary to participate in competitive swimming. Descriptions of mechanics, teaching progressions, and helpful hints for starting,

---

[1]To obtain assistance for teaching nonswimmers to swim, review *A Practical Guide for Teaching the Mentally Retarded to Swim.* Washington, D.C.: AAHPER (1201 - 16th Street, N.W.), 1969, $2.00.

finishing, turning, swimming in lanes, and start-and finishing relays are provided.

Fun activities create enthusiasm, make practice fun, and allow youngsters to swim in less formal situations. Conclude each practice session with five to ten minutes of games and relays — see that all youngsters participate. In Cycles 1-7 incorporate warm-down as a part of fun activities. In Cycles 8-10 warm-down is provided through a relaxed swim, float, glide, easy bobbing, or rhythmic breathing. Do not confine fun activities to the end of practice; be flexible and use them as a change of pace and to help individual swimmers.

Cycles 1-7 are basic in nature and include information and activities designed to help youngsters learn and master fundamentals of competitive swimming. In early practice sessions, encourage youngsters to participate in both crawl and backstroke activities to determine — or help them determine — their best stroke and event. In Cycles 8 and 9 swimmers concentrate on specific events; all continue to practice the relay. Cycle 10 provides helpful hints for final practice sessions before actual competition and includes suggestions for premeet procedures and warm-up activities, workouts stressing speed and quality of performance, and simulated competitive activities; relay teams practice as units to perfect touch-offs and timing.

In using the cycles —

- Work individually with each youngster every practice session to develop a pleasant relationship and show each youngster that you are interested in him.

- Make mental and written notes on strengths and weaknesses of individual swimmers as you observe each in practice.

- Review all cycles before meeting swimmers for the first time to obtain insights into progressions, sequences, methods, procedures, and relationships between successive cycles.

- Strive to develop team spirit and togetherness from the very first practice session. Although most swimming events are contested among individuals, coaches who fail to capitalize on team aspects of this sport are losing one of the most effective ways to build *esprit de corps*. Provide opportunities for swimmers to work together, to help each other, and to root for one another in practice, simulated competition, and actual meets. Develop a spirit of comradeship and togetherness to promote friendships that will endure long after youngsters are through with competitive swimming.

Try a variety of approaches to encourage swimmers to practice hard —

- Post latest times for each swimmer in each event; emphasize improvement and illustrate with charts, graphs, and pictures.

- Award patches, certificates, ribbons at appropriate times for significant improvement.

- Place pictures of youngsters who make greatest improvement each week or month on bulletin board.

- Post names of winners of each event in intrasquad competition on bulletin board.

- Set up squad distance swimming goals such as swimming the distance from Cleveland to Detroit or New York to Los Angeles; put a map on the bulletin board and chart progress. Keep records of number of miles each youngster swims for 10, 50, or even 100 mile clubs.

- Establish a weekly or monthly honor roll of swimmers who make outstanding progress or reach specified goals during the week or month.

- Set up a *Hall of Fame* for superlative performances such as setting new Special Olympics records, winning local, state, or national championships, or placing in two events.

- Recognize individuals whose sportsmanship, behavior, and conduct exemplify the highest ideals of the Olympic tradition.

Most successful coaches are good swimmers and constantly strive to improve their own swimming ability. A qualified lifeguard, one fully certified in first aid, should be at pool site whenever the team practices. All coaches and assistants should know the basic principles of lifesaving and first aid including mouth-to-mouth resuscitation.

Landlubber's Loosen-up — *Warm-up*

Helpful Hints

- Start every practice session for all swimmers with planned warm-up activities.

- Arrange practice sessions so that time used for *Landlubber's Loosen-up* does not take away from actual pool time.

- Complete warm-up activities before swimmers enter the water.

- Use warm-up activities to prepare each swimmer for vigorous activity when he enters the water.

- Include *at least* one activity from each of the three listed categories in every practice session.

- Follow suggested sequences and incorporate appropriate variations for these activities (pp. 10-20).

Bending and Stretching

Move the trunk and upper body forward, backward, or sideward.

Wing Stretcher (p. 10)
Body Bender (p. 10)
Trunk Twister (p. 11)
Wood Chopper (p. 11)
Standing Elbow Knee Touch (p. 12)

Flexibility

Stretch the front and back of the thighs.

Touchdown (p. 12)
Windmill (p. 13)
Sitting Windmill (p. 13)
Sitting Crossover (p. 14)
Inverted Bridge/Arch (p. 15)

Abdominal Endurance

Use abdominal muscles over longer periods of time.

See Saw (p. 19)
Sit-Ups (p. 19)
Bent Leg Sit-Ups (p. 20)
Curl (p. 20)
V-Up (p. 20)

Five Fathoms — *Conditioning*

A good swimmer must be in excellent physical condition. He must develop and maintain high levels of endurance, strength, speed, power, coordination, balance, agility, and flexibility. Hard work and stick-to-itiveness are needed for continuous improvement in these basic components of fitness. (Conditioning exercises and activities are described and discussed in detail in the section on conditioning and fitness, pp. 6-40). A special aquatic routine, *Five Fathoms*, has been designed specifically to help condition and prepare swimmers for competition; each of the exercises is done in the water as described below.

ARM CIRCLES

Stand in water at shoulder level.

Extend arms to each side just below surface of water.

Make small vigorous circles with arms.

Move arms forward and then backward.

Variations:

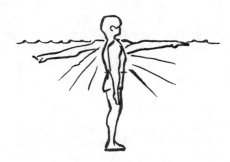

Stand in water at chest level with hands against sides of legs.

Swing one arm forward and one backward in a continuing alternate manner; bring each arm just to surface of water; keep elbows straight.

or

Bring both arms forward to shoulder level and back.

Stand in water at chest level with hands against sides of legs.

Extend arms from sides to surface of water at shoulder level.

Bring hands back to sides and continue pattern.

- Stand in water at chest level.
- Windmill both arms alternately through the water imitating a swimmer doing a crawl (back) stroke.

FLEXIBILITY

Stand in water at shoulder level and put one shoulder or the back against a side of the pool.

Balance on one foot and bring the opposite knee toward the chest.

Grasp elevated leg just below the knee with both hands and pull it gently into the chest stretching muscles of hip, thigh, and back.

Release and repeat with other leg.

Variation:

Lift the leg a given number of times before repeating with other leg.

KICKING

Hold onto the edge of pool with both hands and extend both legs behind.

Move legs alternately without bending knees (flutter kick); each foot travels only 12 to 18 inches.

Variation:

Kick while on the back.

STROKING

Hook toes into gutter (overflow) and assume front glide (prone, stomach down) position.

Move arms alternately imitating a swimmer doing a crawl stroke.

Variations:

Hook toes over pool or lane divider or have a partner hold legs.

Move arms while on back.

BOBBING

Stand in chest-deep water.

Take a breath and submerge.

Squat and exhale while on bottom of pool.

Straighten legs, regain standing position, and repeat pattern.

Helpful Hints:

Challenge swimmers to work hard to become physically fit and aqua-conditioned so that they will be better swimmers. Add interesting variations to each of the Five Fathoms:

- Do more repetitions of each activity in a specific time.
- Increase intensity and speed at which each activity is done.
- Provide resistance for swimmer to overcome as he performs various activities. Use weight cuffs on ankles, legs, wrists, or arms; have youngster wear a weighted vest or weight belt of some type; kick against an object such as a partner's hand or a tightly held pool divider.

	Cycle 1	Cycle 2
Warm-up	Spend 1 min. on each phase of *Land Lubber's Loosen-up* (pp. 111-112). Run in place 1 min.	Spend 1 min. 15 sec. on each phase of *Land Lubber's Loosen-up* (pp. 111-112). Run in place 1 min. 15 sec.
Conditioning	Spend 30 sec. on each exercise of *Five Fathoms* (pp. 112-113). Relax 2 min. Repeat each of Five Fathoms 30 sec.	Spend 45 sec. on each exercise of *Five Fathoms* (pp. 112-113). Relax 1 ½ -min. Repeat each exercise of *Five Fathoms* 45 sec.
Stroke work and Special Fundamentals	*Swim and Show* Give each youngster an opportunity to show how well he can swim to determine strengths and weaknesses. Remember, each youngster in this program can swim. Avoid competition at this point—let youngsters do their thing, get to know you, and have fun as you see what each can do. Look for indications that some youngsters may be better suited for crawl and others for backstroke. *Games* (pp. 137-138). Use games and other fun activities to give youngsters a chance to swim and show. *Relays* (pp. 137-138). Use regular, conventional, novelty, original relays, and drills made into relays to give youngsters additional chances to swim and show.	Divide time so one-third is spent on *arm work*, one-third on *leg work*, and one-third on *breathing activities*. Select drills, activities, and approaches according to ability levels, strengths, and weaknesses of each swimmer. At this stage, be sure each youngster practices both strokes. Crawl: p. 120 / p. 121 / p. 122 Backstroke: p. 125 / p. 126 / p. 127 Emphasize swimming in lanes (p. 128). No further mention or special attention will be given to swimming in lanes—stress swimming in lanes in every practice session. Use remaining time for swimming lengths in lanes; emphasize *good form*. Swim one all out (full speed) length in stroke of choice.
Fun Activities	*Flutter, Fin, and Form* Swim widths of pool, kick widths, swim widths using arms only; time widths involving entire stroke, arms or legs only. Use same activities and approaches for lengths of pool; observe how youngsters stay in lanes and swim in a straight line.	Include games, relays, and other fun activities at end of *every* practice session (pp. 137-138). Be sure final activity is slow, easy, and relaxing. Include relays as one type of fun activity at the end of every practice session so youngsters will have opportunities to develop understanding of concepts, mechanics, and procedures of swimming relays.

> *Some men preceve things as they are and say, "Why." I dream things that never were and say, "Why not?"*
>
> Robert Kennedy

	Cycle 3	**Cycle 4**
Warm-up	Spend 1 ½ min. on each phase of Land Lubber's Loosen-up (pp. 111-112). Run in place 1 ½ min.	Spend 1 min. 45 sec. on each phase of Land Lubber's Loosen-up (pp. 111-112). Run in place 1 min. 45 sec.
Conditioning	Spend 1 min. on each exercise of *Five Fathoms* (pp. 112-113). Relax 1 ½ min. Repeat each exercise of *Five Fathoms* 45 sec.	Spend 1 ½ min. on each exercise of *Five Fathoms* (pp. 112-113). Relax 30 sec. Bob 2 min.

Stroke work and Special Fundamentals	Swim length of pool stressing controlled speed —*maintain good form with good speed.* Return to start (size of the pool will determine whether swimmers stay in water and return in a rest lane or get out of pool and walk back over the deck). Continue this pattern—swim a length and return to start until each swimmer completes 6 swimming lengths. Alternate swimming lengths so each youngster completes three lengths using each stroke.
	
	    Crawl p. 119 *Backstroke* pp. 123-124
	
	Use additional time to give swimmers opportunities to work on specific form weaknesses in both strokes— —arm drills, leg drills, and breathing activities.
	
	  Crawl *Backstroke*
	  Arms
	  p. 120 p. 125
	  Legs
	  p. 121 p. 126
	  Breathing
	  p. 122 p. 127
	
	Starts pp. 129-132 p. 135
	
	Work on the mechanics of getting into the water efficiently and effectively; stress progression, not use of starting commands at this point.
	
	Swim an all-out (full speed) length in stroke of choice; return immediately to start and swim another all out length using same stroke.
		Work on refining and improving all phases of stroke form; use drills and other specific activities for this purpose. Spend some time stressing *arms,* some on *legs,* and some on *breathing.* Continue to include both strokes for all swimmers.
		
		  Crawl *Backstroke*
		  p. 120 *Arms*
		       p. 125
		  p. 121 *Legs*
		       p. 126
		  p. 122 *Breathing*
		       p. 127
		
		Swim as many lengths as possible in 10 min.; swim is not continuous as youngsters get out of water and walk back to starting point or use rest stroke or float in lane for this purpose depending on size and type of pool. Emphasize form and skill but strive to increase speed and tempo. Let youngster swim stroke of choice.
		
		Review mechanics of start. Introduce starting commands with whistle or gun. Divide time equally between the two strokes.
		
		  Crawl *Backstroke*
		  pp. 131-132 p. 135
		
		Introduce turns. p. 133 ———
		
		Swim a timed 25 yds. or length in stroke of choice at end of each practice session in this cycle.
		
		Introduce concept of swimming against another youngster or youngsters by having two or more swimmers race length of pool; keep competition as even as possible by pairing youngsters of near equal ability.

Fun Activities	Include games, relays, and other fun activities at the end of *every* practice session (pp. 137-138). Be sure final activity is slow, easy, and relaxing. Include relays as one type of fun activity at the end of every practice session so youngsters have opportunities to develop understanding of concepts, mechanics, and procedures of swimming relays.	Use games, relays, and other fun activities to end practice. Be sure final activity is slow, easy and relaxing. Include relays as part of fun activities in every practice session. pp. 137-138

	Cycle 5	**Cycle 6**
Warm-up	Spend 2 min. on each phase of *Land Lubber's Loosen-up* (pp. 111-112). Run in place 2 min.	Spend 1 min. on each phase of *Land Lubber's Loosen-up* (pp. 111-112). Run in place 1 min. Repeat pattern — 1 min. of each phase of *Land Lubber's Loosen-up* followed by 1 min. run in place.
Conditioning	Spend 2 min. on each exercise of *Five Fathoms* (pp. 112-113).	Spend 2 min. on each exercise of *Five Fathoms* (pp. 112-113).
Stroke work and Special Fundamentals	Emphasize phase of stroke — *arms, legs, breathing* — in need of greatest attention; spend sometime on all phases of stroke of choice. *Crawl* — Arms p. 120, Legs p. 121, Breathing p. 122, General Form p. 119. *Backstroke* — Arms p. 125, Legs p. 126, Breathing p. 127, General Form pp. 123-124. Swim 2 lengths; relax; continue pattern — two lengths followed by rest — until 5 repetitions have been completed; continue using stroke of choice. Review *starting* mechanics and procedures in stroke of choice. pp. 131-132 p. 135 Review turns (p. 133). Introduce *finish* p. 132 p. 136 procedures and techniques in both strokes. Swim a timed 50 yds. crawl or 2 lengths at end of each practice session in this cycle. Have youngsters swim 50 yds. with 2 or more swimming with or racing against each other; keep competition as even as possible by pairing youngsters of near equal ability.	Spend sometime on form drills stressing individual needs of each swimmer but including *all* phases of stroke of choice. *Crawl* — Arms p. 120, Legs p. 121, Breathing p. 122, General Form p. 119, Starts pp. 129-132, Turns p. 133. *Backstroke* — Arms p. 125, Legs p. 126, Breathing p. 127, General Form pp. 123-124, Starts p. 135, Finish p. 136. Swim as many lengths as possible in 10 min. — emphasize speed while maintaining good form in stroke of choice. Swim an all-out (full speed) 50 yards or 2 lengths; relax for 2-3 min. and swim an all out 25 yds. or length; use stroke of choice. Review and practice *starts, finish,* and *turns.* Swim an all-out 50 yds. or 2 lengths; relax for 2-3 min. and swim an all out 25 yds. or 1 length; use stroke of choice.
Fun Activities	Use games, relays, and other fun activities (pp 137-138) to end practice. Be sure fun activity is slow, easy, and relaxing. Include relays as part of fun activities in every practice session.	Use games, relays, and other fun activities (pp 137-138) to end practice. Be sure final activity is slow, easy, and relaxing. Include relays as part of fun activities in every practice session.

	Cycle 7	Cycle 8

Warm-up	Do *Land-Lubber's Loosen-up* and run in place as follows:
	
	    1 min. *bend and stretch* (p. 112).
	
	    1 min. run in place.
	
	    1 min. *flexibility* (p. 112).
	
	    1 min. run in place.
	
	    1 min. *abdominal endurance* (p. 112).
	
	    1 min. run in place.
		Provide each swimmer with opportunities to develop his own warm-up procedures for actual competition; include all skills required for each youngster's competitive event; have initial warm-up activities out of water before moving into pool; use specific activities for *arms, legs, total stroke, start, finish, turn, relay starts* and *finishes;* increase speed gradually and in final portions of warm-up include all-out (full speed) swimming.

Conditioning	Spend 2 min. on each exercise of *Five Fathoms* (pp. 112-113).	

	Cycle 7	Cycle 8
Stroke work and Special Fundamentals	Entire workout in stroke of choice. Use special leg drills. *Crawl* p. 121 *Backstroke* p. 126 Swim 50 yds. or 2 lengths; relax 2 to 3 min. and swim another 50 yds. or 2 lengths. Use special arm drills. p. 120 p. 125 Swim 25 yds. or 1 length; relax for 1 min. p. 119 pp. 123-124 and repeat this pattern—swim 25 yds. or 1 length followed by 1 min. relaxing—3 *more* times. Use special *breathing* drills. p. 122 p. 127 Swim 50 yds. or 2 lengths; relax 2 or 3 min. and swim 25 yds. or 1 length. Review *start, finish,* and *turn* procedures and techniques. *Start* pp. 129-132 p. 135 *Finish* p. 132 p. 136 *Turn* p. 133 —— Swim continuously for 5 min. Swim in all-out (full speed) 50 yds. or 2 lengths. Swim an all-out 25 yds. or 1 length.	*25 yard freestyle and 25 yard backstroke* Start from standing (not regular starting position) at one end of pool; swim 25 yds. or 1 length trying to equal or better best previous time or time youngster hopes to achieve in competition. Relax with rest stroke, float, bob, or tread water for 5 min. Repeat pattern—swim 25 yds. or 1 length as above and relax 5 min. —do total of 4 times. *Relay* All youngsters, including backstroke swimmers, participate. Divide youngsters into teams of 3 or 5 and place as shown on diagram for continuous relay swimming; continue relay until each youngster has completed 5 lengths. *50 yard freestyle* Start from standing position at one end of pool; swim 25 yds. in time equal to desired time for first lap of 50 yd. swim; complete turn and glide to stop. Relax with rest stroke, float, bob, or tread water for 3-4 min. Repeat pattern—swim 25 yds. as above and relax 3-4 min.—do total of 6 to 8 times.
Fun Activities and Warm-down	Use games, relays, and other fun activities (pp 137-138) to end practice. Be sure final activity is slow, easy, and relaxing. Include relays as part of fun activities in every practice session.	End practice with slow, easy, and relaxing swimming or aquatic activity such as form swimming, rhythmic breathing, easy bobbing, floating, or gliding.

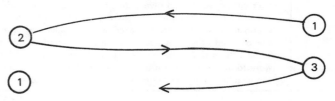

Cycle 9

Warm-up	Continue to experiment with individual warm-up routines so that each swimmer knows exactly what to include in his premeet preparation; too little warm-up and a youngster will not be ready for peak performance; too much warm-up and he loses speed and endurance needed for maximum performance; time warm-up so youngster peaks and is ready for his event when it is called, not before or after. Recognize each swimmer as an individual—each requires different pattern, length, and intensity of warm-up. Review Cycle 8 for additional suggestions regarding premeet warm-up.

Event Workouts

25 yard freestyle and
25 yard backstroke

Swim one-half length between ½ and ¾ speed—sprint (full speed) rest of length; repeat as many times as possible in 10 min.

Use regular start and sprint ¾ length; continue to end of pool maintaining maximum relaxed speed; repeat as many times as possible in 10 min.

Practice gun or whistle starts 10 min.

Swim an all-out (full speed) 25 yd. sprint or 1 length; rest 1 min. and swim another all out 25 or 1 length.

50 yard freestyle

Swim 50 yds. 2-3 sec. slower than best previous time or time youngster hopes to achieve in competition; complete turn and sprint (full speed) an additional ½ to ¾ length.

Relax with rest stroke, float, bob, or tread water 5 min.

Swim 25 yds. 2-3 sec. slower than time desired for first lap of 50 yd. swim; complete turn and sprint second 25 yds.; rest; repeat this pattern 3-4 times.

Practice gun or whistle starts 10 min.

Swim an all-out (full speed) 25 yd. sprint or 1 length; rest 1 min. and swim another all-out 25 or 1 length; be sure to complete turn on each length.

Relay—All youngsters, including backstroke swimmers, participate.

Place youngsters on relay teams making sure individuals who will likely swim together are placed on same teams and in the order they will probably swim.

Practice touch-offs to perfect timing (p. 134).

Have relay competition among various teams; use head-start system (start teams at different times according to ability) to give slower teams a chance and to challenge faster teams.

Warm-down	End practice with slow, easy, and relaxing swimming or aquatic activity such as form swimming, rhythmic breathing, easy bobbing, floating, or gliding.

Cycle 10

Warm-up	Have each youngster use premeet procedures and warm-up activities exactly as he will on meet days. Only minor adjustments in routine developed through Cycles 8 and 9 should now be necessary. Tell youngster time his event will be called and help him determine when to start warm-up so as to be competitively sharp at the right moment.

Event Workouts

Helpful Hints for Final Practice Sessions

Stress speed and quality of performance rather than quantity of work—have youngsters swim at speeds equal to or better than competitive speeds.

Devote time as necessary to any aspect of form, tactics, or strategy needed by youngsters in their competitive events—select appropriate activities, drills, and practice approaches from any of previous cycles that will accomplish these purposes with individual swimmers.

Provide time for relay teams to practice as units to perfect touch-offs and timing.

Plan simulated competitive activities such as *time trials, intrasquad meets,* and *practice meets* with other teams. *Telegraphic* or *mail-a-graphic meets* (each team swims in its own pool; times for each youngster in every event are exchanged by telegram or letter) with teams in other parts of the country can be used effectively. Be careful not to schedule too many competitive activities and guard against holding them too close to meet days. Do not have two actual competitive activities in the same week—work to obtain maximum performances in actual competition not practice meets. Competitive activities can also be used in earlier cycles to add interest, incentive, and to change practice routine and pace.

Warm-down	Be sure each youngster warms-down after actual competition as well as after practice sessions; encourage each to use activities he likes and which are best suited for him.

Crawl Stroke Fundamentals and Teaching Progressions

General Form

The crawl stroke requires coordination of arm and leg movements and breath control. Both the 25 and 50 yard freestyle events are sprints and youngsters must be mentally and physically prepared to go all out in each. Some youngsters may have to approach the 50 yard freestyle as an endurance event until they are conditioned for an all out effort. Regardless of how approached—as a sprint or an endurance event—the time for each lap of the 50 yard freestyle should be approximately the same.

Fundamentals

Keep body as flat and horizontal as possible.

Turn head smoothly from forward position with face in water, to side with face out of water. If swimmer raises his head out of water, his legs may sink and the body lose its horizontal position.

Keep eyes open while face is under water.

Helpful Hints:

- Emphasize good total form at all times, especially when swimmers are tired and near the end of practice sessions.

- Increase speed of widths, lengths, and repetitions in which form is emphasized; *controlled speed* is a key to developing good form.

- Recognize that although several youngsters may have similar difficulties, different steps in a teaching progression may have to be used with each individual. Know and be able to apply each of these steps, but use and apply only those necessary to reach a particular individual. Use different steps to provide the variety, repetition, and review some individuals will need to develop an efficient and effective crawl stroke.

To develop strength and endurance, or to practice general or specific components of form—

Use kick boards for support to practice kicking or arm strokes.

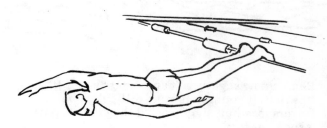

Attach ropes or place pool or lane dividers so youngsters can use them for support while practicing kicking or arm strokes.

Bracket against a pool wall to practice either kicking or arm strokes.

Make swim *trainers or platforms* so youngsters can practice swimming movements on land to develop skill, strength, endurance, and the feel of appropriate patterns.

Arm Action

The arm stroke is an alternating action in which one arm propels or pulls as the other recovers.

Fundamentals

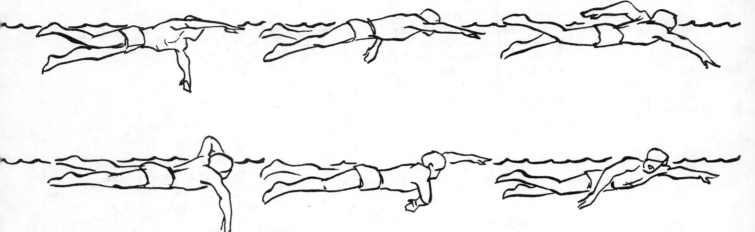

Bend elbow slightly so hand enters water fingertips first. If youngsters have difficulty keeping fingers together, simply ask if they eat soup with a spoon or fork!

Let hand break water and continue below surface. A powerful underwater pull is downward and backward in a direct line beneath body and toward thigh.

Teaching Progression

To teach an individual swimmer appropriate arm action, use methods and procedures from this progression—add your own steps or develop your own progressions.

- Use swim trainers or platforms on land so youngsters get the feel of arm movements.
- Guide youngster through crawl arm movement so he feels the appropriate action; do this in water or out of pool.
- Stand in shallow water and move arms appropriately.
- Stand with shoulders beneath surface of water and practice appropriate arm action.
- Walk across pool making arm movements; go from shallow to chest depth.
- Walk, drag toes on bottom of pool, and do crawl arm stroke.
- Hook toes in gutter (overflow), assume front glide (prone, stomach down) position, and do crawl arm stroke.
- Hook toes or place waist over pool or lane divider and do crawl arm stroke.

Let elbow lead as it breaks surface of water. Many swim sprinters gain speed by bringing arm through flat with little bend in elbow as it breaks surface of water.

- Have partner hold legs while swimmer does arm stroke.
- Support legs on kickboard or other flotation device and practice crawl arm movements.
- Glide across pool using crawl arm movements.
- Practice crawl arm movements with added resistance such as arm cuff or partner pushing against arms..

Helpful Hint:
- Hold hands or some object in front of swimmer so that as he alternately reaches for them, he approximates crawl arm action.

Leg Action

Kicking involves upward and downward movements of the legs in which the heels just break the surface of the water and then go 12 to 18 inches under water. The key to a strong flutter kick is power generated from the hips.

Fundamentals

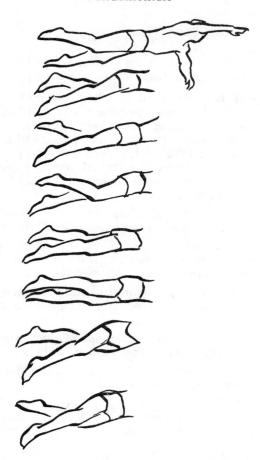

Keep knees and legs straight for whip-like action.

Point toes throughout kick.

Ask a swimmer who tends to bend his knees excessively to keep his feet under water which generally results in the youngster straightening his knees.

Teaching Progression

Various devices and teaching techniques can be used to help swimmers develop efficient and effective leg action. Activities can be conducted out of the pool or in the water to enable youngsters to generate more power through a vigorous and well-coordinated flutter kick.

- Use swim trainers or platforms on land so youngsters get the feel of appropriate leg movements.
- Practice kicking while lying or moving on gym scooters.
- Lie across a chair (bench, piano bench, stool, bed) and practice kicking.
- Guide youngster through crawl leg movements so he feels appropriate action; do this in water.
- Bracket against a pool wall and practice kicking.
- Hold onto or place waist over pool or lane divider and kick.
- Have partner hold hands while swimmer kicks.
- Support arms on kickboard or other flotation device and practice kicking.
- Glide across pool using leg movements.
- Practice flutter kick with hands held at sides; make movement throughout water more difficult and challenging by holding weighted objects in hands.
- Practice leg movements with added resistance such as leg cuff or partner pushing against legs.

Breathing Action

Breathing is accomplished by turning the face to the left or right each time that arm comes out of the water; always breathe on the same side. Inhale, turn the face back into the water as that arm comes forward, and then exhale under water. Breathing should at all times be natural and normal; avoid gulping air or excessive exhaling.

Fundamentals

Turn head until mouth clears surface of water.

Inhale while mouth is above surface of water.

Breathe to side and not to sky.

Turn head out of water on one side only.

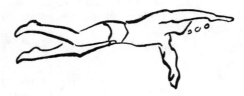

Exhale while face is in water.

Keep eyes open while face is under water.

Breathe in a rhythmical pattern.

Teaching Progression

Breathing techniques can be taught and reinforced in the following ways—

- Use *wet ears* drill in which swimmer turns his head to side, keeping ear on that side in water. Bring face back into water and then rotate head to other side, keeping that ear in water; inhale when face and nose are out of water. Note side on which breathing seems to be easier and encourage youngster to breathe on that side.
- Stand with shoulders beneath water and practice coordinated head and breathing movements.
- Stand with shoulders beneath water and coordinate breathing and arm movements.
- Walk across pool coordinating breathing and arm movements; go from shallow to chest depth.
- Walk, drag toes on bottom of pool, and coordinate breathing and arm movements.
- Support legs on kickboard or other flotation device while coordinating head and breathing movements.
- Glide across pool coordinating head and breathing movements.
- Swim one (two, three, four) stroke(s) emphasizing coordinated breathing and arm movements.
- Swim for various distances emphasizing coordinated breathing and arm movements for longer periods of time, over greater distances, and at faster paces.

Backstroke Fundamentals and Teaching Progressions

General Form

Like the crawl, backstroke swimming requires a strong, coordinated stroke and a powerful kick. Since the face is up and the mouth always clear of the water, breathing is less difficult and swimmers are less likely to swallow water than when they use the crawl stroke. The 25 yard backstroke is a sprint and swimmers must be prepared mentally and conditioned physically to go all out through the entire race; maximum speed requires good form—

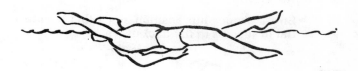

Fundamentals

Maintain body in as flat and horizontal position as possible.

Arch back slightly with belly button up.

Keep head pillowed back in a comfortable position in water.

Teaching Progression

While every youngster in the program knows how to swim, some may have had little if any experience with the backstroke. Therefore, it may be necessary to introduce the beginning fundamentals of the backstroke.

Helpful Hint:

- Stand in back of youngsters who have difficulty so as to support their shoulders until they acquire the confidence to float alone.

Back Float

Stand in waist-deep water with feet 6 to 8 inches apart.

Squat down as if to sit in a chair until shoulders are below surface of water.

Keep hands under water and stretch them to sides with palms up.

Tilt head back, keep ears in water, and look directly at sky or ceiling.

Raise hips as close to surface as possible and move into a back float position.

Keep hips at surface; it makes little difference if toes are above water.

Return to standing position by dropping chin forward, drawing knees toward chest, and bringing hands down and forward.

Back Glide

Helpful Hint:

- Stress proper hip position since this is essential to success in the backstroke.

Place both feet against pool wall or one foot against wall and one on bottom of pool; stay in shallow water until glide has been learned.

Hold deck, overflow, or side with both hands; place head back with ears in water. Emphasize correct head position—if it is tilted back too far, water may wash over face.

Variations:

Remove hands from deck, overflow, or side, straighten knees slowly, and push away from wall.

Keep hands against sides of thighs.

Devices and helpful hints described under *Teaching Progressions, Crawl Stroke Fundamentals* (pp. 119-122) can be adapted and applied to backstroke.

Squat down as if doing a back float.

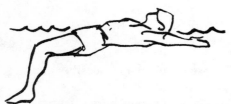

Push back hard with head toward shallow water.

Press stomach against pool wall.

Stand straight like a soldier; extend arms overhead, take a deep breath, hold it, push off bottom, and slide back through water lowering arms to sides for balance.

Arm Action

The arm stroke consists of an alternating action in which one arm enters the water as the other recovers. Coordinated arm movements produce most of the power and generate a lot of the speed in the backstroke.

Fundamentals

Lift left shoulder slightly over water; bring left arm out of water and away from body over water so water doesn't splash into face.

Put left hand in water in advance of head and in line with or just wide of shoulder line at about 1 o'clock.

Keep hand and arm in line with pull.

Start movements of right shoulder and right arm as left hand enters water; right hand enters water at about 11 o'clock.

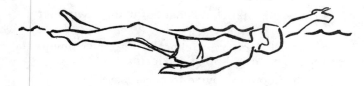

Pull in a semicircular sideward sweep, bringing hand under water directly toward hips.

Turn hand as it approaches thigh so back of hand leads out of water, little finger first.

Lift arm and move it back in a sideward semi-circular motion to point where it enters water.

Coordinate so one hand enters water as other is leaving it.

Teaching Progression

A variety of approaches and procedures can be used with individual youngsters to help them develop the mechanics of effective and efficient backstroke arm action. Select steps from the following progression to fit needs of individual swimmers—add your own steps or develop your own progressions.

- Guide youngster through backstroke arm movements so he feels the appropriate action; do this in water or out of pool.
- Lie across a chair (bench, piano bench, stool, bed) and practice arm action.
- Stand in shallow water and move arms appropriately; move to increasing depths.
- Walk across pool doing backstroke arm movements; go from shallow to chest depth.
- Walk, drag heels on bottom of pool, and perform backstroke arm movements.
- Hold heels on gutter (overflow), assume back glide (supine, stomach up) position, and perform appropriate arm movements.
- Hold heels or place small of back over pool or lane divider and perform backstroke arm action.
- Have partner hold legs while swimmer does arm stroke.
- Support legs on kickboard or other flotation device and practice backstroke arm movements.
- Add arm action to back float and back glide.
- Practice arm movements with added resistance such as arm cuff or partner pushing against arms.

Leg Action

Kicking involves upward and downward movements of the legs in which the toes go to a point just under surface of water and heels come just to the surface. A strong flutter kick provides speed, momentum, and helps a swimmer maintain good balance and body position.

Fundamentals

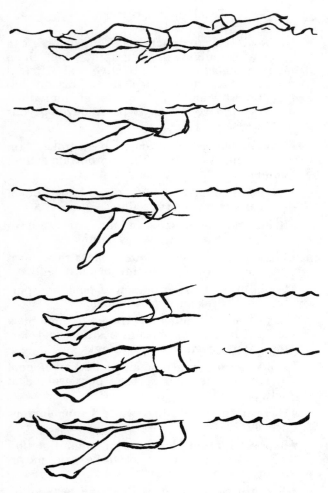

Keep kick shallow and within depth of body.

Point toes throughout with feet turned in naturally.

Keep knees straight and kick from hips.

Teaching Progression

No single approach will guarantee that every swimmer will successfully learn backstroke leg action. An effective instructor uses many devices to provide for individual differences and needs. A variety of activities, drills, and techniques can be used to help youngsters develop a strong, well-coordinated backstroke flutter kick:

- Practice kicking while lying or moving on gym scooters.
- Lie across a chair (bench, piano bench, box, stool, bed) and practice kicking.
- Guide youngster through backstroke leg movement so he feels appropriate action; do this in water or out of pool.
- Bracket against a pool wall and practice kicking.
- Hold onto or place small of back over pool or lane divider and kick.
- Have partner hold hands while swimmer kicks.
- Support arms on kickboard or other floatation device and practice kicking.
- Hold flotation device to chest, scull, and flutter kick.
- Add flutter kick to back float and back glide.
- Practice flutter kick with hands held at sides or arms extended and held over head; make movement through water more difficult and challenging by holding weighted objects in hands.
- Practice leg movements with added resistance such as leg cuff or partner pushing against legs.

Breathing Action

Breathing is less difficult in the backstroke than in other strokes because the face is up and the mouth always clear of the water. Breathing should at all times be natural and normal; avoid inhaling or exhaling excessive amounts of air.

Fundamentals

Teaching Progression

Generally, little difficulty is encountered in teaching breath control and breathing mechanics for the backstroke. However, for youngsters who have difficulty with backstroke breathing, or to provide additional opportunities to practice this part of the stroke, some special attention may be necessary.

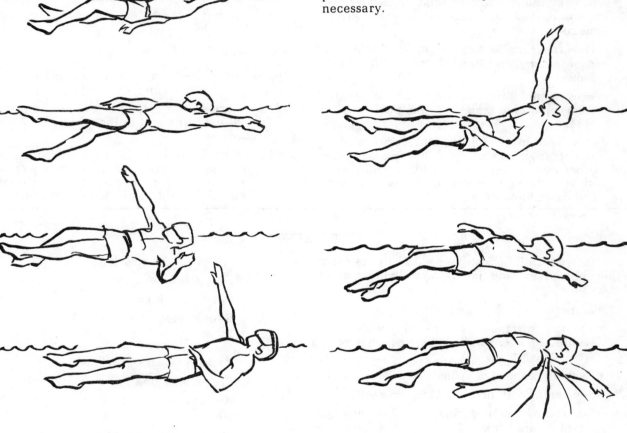

Use elementary backstroke as means of developing effective breath control and breathing mechanics.

- Float on back, scull, and breathe naturally and normally.
- Glide on back, scull, and breathe naturally and normally.
- Float on back, flutter kick, and breathe naturally and normally.
- Glide on back, flutter kick, and breathe naturally and normally.
- Combine scull and flutter kick with natural and normal breathing.

127

Swimming in Lanes

The shortest distance between two points is a straight line! Both freestyle and backstroke swimmers must learn to swim in a straight line and to stay in lanes. Developing an understanding of this concept and practicing the skills can be incorporated into virtually every aspect of each practice session.

- Keep lane dividers up during different phases of practice sessions.
- Walk (run, hop, jump, gallop, skip, slide) in straight lines and through a lane; vary the direction so youngsters move forward, backward, sideward.
- Use exploratory activities and problem solving approaches; ask questions and pose problems such as:
  - ✓ How fast can you move from one end of the pool to the other? Can you move still faster? Slower?
  - ✓ How many different ways can you move from one end (side) of the pool to the other?
  - ✓ Can you move (glide, kick, arm stroke, swim) from one end of the pool to the other in a straight line? Without getting out of your lane? Can you go faster than the last time? Slower?
  - ✓ Can you go underwater and stay in a straight line? Stay in your own lane?
  - ✓ Can you go underwater from one side of the pool to the other and stay in a straight line? Can you go across and back underwater and return to starting point?
- Place objects on bottom of pool so youngster must go in a straight line to retrieve them.
- Use various games and relays (pp 137-138) in which youngsters must stay in lanes or swim in straight lines; devise your own games and relays for these purposes; encourage youngsters to make-up activities.
- Adapt various drills, swim training lengths, and use other practice activities to help improve these skills.

Helpful Hints:

- Use some object on pool deck or mark in the pool as a beacon to help stay on course.
- Use markings on bottom of pool to help stay in a straight line and in the middle of a lane in crawl.
- Select markings or objects such as lights on ceiling, cloud formations, or other objects in the pool environment to help stay in a straight line and in the middle of a lane in backstroke.

Interval Training

Interval training can be used to fit the condition, objectives, and needs of individual swimmers by —

- Increasing number of repetitions.
- Varying distances swam—one width, two widths, one length, two lengths, 25 yds., 50 yds., 100 yds.
- Regulating speed of swim.
- Shortening rest intervals between swims.
- Controlling action during rest or recovery interval—walk, float, bob, tread; discourage sitting or lying down during rest or recovery intervals.

Emphasis in interval training is upon swimming speed and pace so timing widths, laps, and recovery intervals can become an important part of these activities. Examples of interval training routines that might be done following a thorough warm-up are:

Crawl stroke two laps.

Rest stroke one lap.

Bob two minutes.

Repeat pattern three or four times.

Backstroke kick two laps.

Rest stroke one lap.

Backstroke arm stroke one lap.

Tread water one minute.

Repeat pattern three or four times.

Crawl stroke 50 yds. 2 sec. slower than best or goal time.

Float or rest stroke 2 min.

Repeat pattern three times.

Freestyle Tactics and Teaching Progressions

Dive

The start of 25 and 50 yard freestyle races can be either from in the water or by diving from the deck. When youngsters dive they accelerate faster and actually shorten the distance they have to swim. Basic mechanics should be stressed at all steps and levels to teach the dive effectively.

Tactics

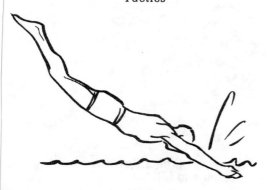

Extend arms so they lead the body and enter water first.

Keep head between arms with hands together and arms in line with ears.

Enter water with legs fully extended and in line with rest of body.

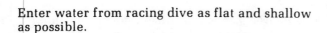

Enter water from racing dive as flat and shallow as possible.

Teaching Progression

There are many activities for teaching a racing dive—

Jump into water feet first.

Add variations such as tuck, one leg tuck, squat, *cannon ball*—who can make the biggest splash? —pike, straddle, jump-turns, and other fun ways.

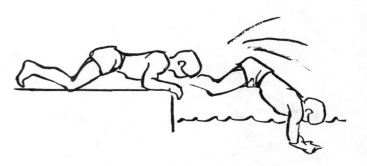

Introduce *seal dive* where youngster takes prone position near edge of pool and simply slides into the water head first.

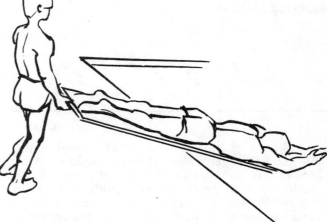

Slide into water from a 2 x 8 plank.

Make task easier or more difficult, more or less challenging, by holding end of the plank at different heights.

Provide opportunities to enter water in different ways—feet first, head first, arms first.

Sit at edge of pool with head down, arms extended, and fall (dive) easily into pool head first.

Move to a semisquat (kneeling, semistanding, standing) position and fall (dive) into pool head first.

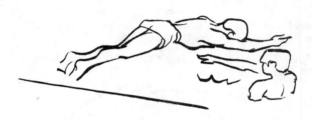

Dive over outstretched arm of another squad member to encourage full extension of the body over water.

Concentrate on shallow entry into water by practicing racing dives.

Helpful Hints:

- Use wide pool steps—not ladders—as an intermediate progression between each of these stages.
- Use targets, such as tires, hoops, or inner tubes to improve diving form and body control.
- Place brightly-colored weighted objects on bottom of pool as points of focus to help improve diving form.

Circuit Training

Circuit training can be used for conditioning or practicing general or specific aquatic skills. Youngsters do a certain number of repetitions at each station or perform for a stipulated time, 10, 15, 20, 30, 45, 60 seconds before moving to the next station. Move in a set pattern on a given signal. The mechanics are simple—

- Set-up stations for kicking, bobbing, treading, bracketing and doing crawl arm stroke, diving for weighted objects, diving, or stroking (complete crawl or backstroke); establish stations to meet needs of individual squad members.
- Assign each youngster to a group—*keep groups small*, two or three ideally.
- Assign each group to a station for designated activity.

Start

Starting commands are: "Swimmers take your marks," followed by a gun or whistle. Devote practice time to getting swimmers accustomed to actual competitive situations. Use a gun or whistle when practicing starts—never start with the verbal command, "Go." Some youngsters may not react appropriately to the sound of a gun or whistle in competition and others may be frightened by the sound, especially in a confined pool where shots may echo and reecho, if they have not been taught to react to the appropriate starting signal.

Tactics

In preparing for competition, stress that on the command, "Take your marks," swimmers—

". . . Take your marks."

Assume a position with toes over edge of pool, feet slightly apart, and knees moderately bent.

Bend trunk forward with head in a comfortable position.

Let arms hang downward or hold them slightly back, depending on individual preference.

Have whole body in relaxed state of readiness.

At the sound of the starting gun or whistle—

Swing arms forward.

Explode from edge of pool by straightening knees and ankles vigorously.

Continue to swing arms foward until they are in line with rest of body.

Keep head well down between arms with upper arms touching ears; thumbs may be locked on impact with water.

Continue in flight as far out over water as possible.

Make entry as shallow and flat as possible.

Begin coordinated action of stroking, kicking, and breathing when body is completely in water.

131

- Assume and hold "Take your marks" position; experiment to find best position for each swimmer.
- Dive on sound of gun or whistle; vary intensity of sound so swimmer reacts to starting signal automatically.
- Dive for distance—get maximum distance from starting dive.
- Dive and glide—get maximum distance from starting dive and following glide.
- Practice short swim sprints such as 5 or 10 yards, or up to one-quarter pool length; challenge swimmers to improve starts by timing these short distances and recording and posting times.
- Have youngsters practice individually then with one or more teammates.

- Try dive competition across pool where swimmers dive and glide one or more widths without stroking.
- Practice dive form—coordinate action from dive to total stroke.

Helpful Hints:

- Encourage swimmers to concentrate on initial diving movement not on listening for starting sound; the best start results from reflex action.
- Emphasize form and controlled speed—with practice, skill, and confidence, speed of coordinated action from dive to stroke will improve.

Finish

The finish is effective when swimmers go at full speed until they touch the end of the pool. Youngsters must practice so they don't slow down as they approach the wall—this should become automatic.

Tactics

Touch wall with fully extended arm.

Touch just above water level; touch below water level rather than taking another stroke.

Touch at full speed without slowing down or altering stroke.

Take another stroke rather than overreaching for the wall; overreaching disrupts rhythm and tends to make swimmer stop and glide into wall.

Develop ability to touch wall with either hand.

Teaching Progression

Many simple activities can be used to help swimmers develop an effective finish.

- Reach for the wall from a stand (walk, drag, glide) without moving the head or other arm.
- Coordinate reach for the wall with breathing and arm movements—stand, walk, drag, glide.
- Swim one (two, three, four) stroke(s) as if it were the last stroke in a race.
- Swim at relaxed pace—on signal or when reaching a specified point in pool, sprint for wall; challenge swimmers to improve finish by timing sprint distances and recording and posting times.
- Have two or more youngsters practice finishing together; follow same sequences outlined for individuals.
- Have two or more youngsters swim several (10, 15) strokes concentrating on the finish.
- Make sure youngsters practice touching at finish with either hand since they never know which arm will be forward when they reach wall.

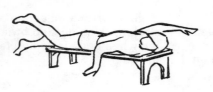

Turns

The 50 yard freestyle is the only Special Olympics swimming event that requires a turn. In a basic turn—

Tactics

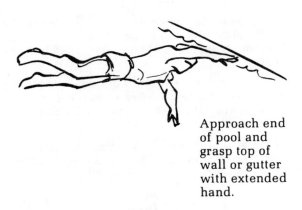

Approach end of pool and grasp top of wall or gutter with extended hand.

Bring knees to chest, place both feet against wall, and turn head and body *away* from extended arm—follow head.

Explode from end of pool by extending knees and pushing feet off wall.

Resume regular swimming stroke as quickly as possible.

Teaching Progression

A progression to practice and develop skill in turning might include—

- Stand and reach for end of pool with arm—complete turn.
- Walk and reach for end of pool with arm—complete turn.
- Glide and reach for end of pool—complete turn.
- Swim a few strokes and reach for end of pool—complete turn.
- Swim at relaxed pace—on signal or when reaching a specified point in pool, sprint for wall, complete turn, sprint until next signal or back to original specified point, and then revert to relaxed pace.
- Swim at racing speed and practice complete turn.
- Have two or more youngsters practice turns together; follow same sequences outlined for individuals.
- Try turn competition across pool where swimmers dive and glide a width making turn without stroking; let youngsters sprint back to starting side after completing turn.
- Have two or more youngsters swim several strokes and turn—see who completes turn first.
- Make sure youngsters practice turning both right and left since they never know which arm will be forward when they reach end of pool.

> *Learning is best accomplished with laughter, adventure, and a sense of triumph.*

133

Relay Fundamentals and Teaching Progressions

Fundamentals

Most relay teams consist of individuals who participate in one of the freestyle events as well as those who swim only the relay. Training procedures and techniques for individual events are appropriate for relay specialists since all freestyle swimmers should spend time on relay fundamentals in each practice session. However, as time for actual competition approaches, additional and specific attention to relay fundamentals, techniques, and strategy must be incorporated into practice sessions. Coaches must teach relay fundamentals as well as develop teamwork since incoming and outgoing swimmers must function as coordinated units.

Set up relay teams keeping these points in mind:

- Swimmers must work well together; if two or more youngsters are nearly equal in ability, select the one who gets along best with other members of relay team.

- Timing is essential so swimmers must learn to work with teammates who preceed and succeed them.

- Practice makes perfect so relay teams must frequently practice together as units.

- Backstroke swimmers should not be overlooked as possible members of relay teams.

Coaches should be flexible in determining who swims in what position on a relay team. A possible order:

- *Lead-off*—best starter; often second fastest swimmer.

- *Second*—slowest or most inexperienced swimmer.

- *Third*—guttiest swimmer—the one who can come from behind.

- *Anchor*—fastest swimmer—and best finisher.

Other combinations to consider in setting up relay teams include—

- Swim the two fastest first and second to get a big lead to inspire better performances from numbers three and four.

- Swim the fastest first, particularly a good starter, and anchor the second fastest.

- Place the fastest second and he will often compete against other teams' weakest swimmers.

Be flexible in setting up the order and experiment to see which procedure provides the fastest time and smoothest arrangement for the team.

Teaching Progression

In practicing relays, make sure swimmers don't start too soon or delay the takeoff on second, third, and fourth legs. Some ways to practice touch-offs include:

- Have incoming swimmer touch the wall real hard—slap it; coach outgoing swimmer to look, listen, and react to sound of the slap.

- Have outgoing swimmer focus his eyes on the wall below him so he can see and react to incoming teammate's hand as it touches the wall.

- Have outgoing swimmer note when incoming teammate is a few strokes from the end of the pool in order to know when to take the ready position.

Include additional diving and starting practice for members of relay teams. Set up a variety of fun activities to practice relay skills:

- Two man relays in which one and two swim against three and four or two and three against one and four.

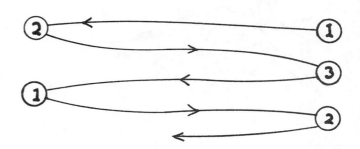

- Three man continuous relays where two swimmers (1 and 3) start at one end of the pool and a third (2) at the other. Relay continues as 1 touches off 2, 2 touches off 3, 3 touches off 1, continuing in this manner for a specified number of laps or time. This pattern can be used with five or seven swimmers.

- Cross pool relays involving teams of four, six, or eight.

- Intrasquad relays.

- Age medley relays.

Don't let the best you have ever done be the standard for the rest of your life.

134

Backstroke Tactics and Teaching Progressions

Start

Tactics

The start of the backstroke is in the water with swimmers facing and holding wall or starting blocks; feet are placed firmly against the starting wall. Starting commands are: "Swimmers take your marks," followed by a gun or whistle. Devote practice time to get swimmers accustomed to actual competitive situations. Use a gun or whistle when practicing starts—never start with the verbal command, "Go." Some youngsters may not react appropriately to the sound of a gun or whistle in competition and others may be frightened by the sound, especially in a confined pool area where shots echo and reecho, if they have not been taught to act and react to the appropriate starting signal.

Practice Progression

- Hold onto gutter or overflow, place one foot low on wall, keep other foot on bottom of pool, and start; increase height of wall foot as swimmer progresses.
- Place both feet low on wall as above and practice start; bring feet gradually higher on wall to get swimmer in suitable position.
- Have a strong teammate act as human starting blocks with swimmer using partner's ankles for support.
- Assume and hold "Take your marks" position; experiment to find best position for each swimmer.
- Start on sound of gun or whistle; vary intensity of sound so swimmer reacts to starting signal automatically.
- Start for distance—get maximum distance from start to total stroke.
- Emphasize form and controlled speed—with practice, skill, and confidence, speed of coordinated action from start to stroke will increase.
- Practice short swim sprints such as 5 or 10 yards or up to one-quarter pool length; challenge swimmers to improve starts by timing these short distances and recording and posting times.
- Have youngsters practice individually, then with one or more teammates.

Helpful Hint:

- Encourage swimmers to concentrate on initial starting movement not on listening for starting sound; the best start results from reflex action.

Teaching Progression

To start in the backstroke, simply push-off, glide, and begin coordinated arm and leg action before losing mementum obtained from the initial push. If swimmers start the coordinated arm and leg action too soon, they lose benefit of the explosive push; if too late, momentum decreases.

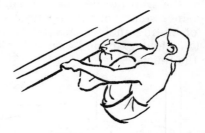

Hold starting rail or wall with both hands about shoulder width apart.

Place feet on wall; keep body in tuck position with feet slightly apart. "...Take your marks."

Raise feet high enough on wall to obtain maximum thrust—go out, not down; rules require that part of body must be in water.

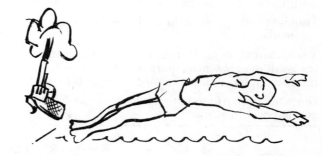

Straighten legs against wall so as to make a backward dive.

Throw both arms backward and stretch body out over water for greater acceleration.

Explode from wall or blocks.

Begin arm and leg action so as to gain maximum benefit from coordinated starting movements.

Finish

The finish is effective when swimmers go full speed until they touch the end of the pool. This must be practiced constantly, even when it becomes automatic. Rules require that a swimmer be on his back when he touches. Work with youngsters to develop the ability to finish fast and reach for the wall on the final stroke. Make haste slowly since some youngsters may be timid and afraid of hitting their heads on the wall; show them that their extended arm will hit first and cushion the finish.

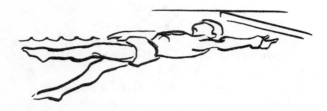

Touch wall with fully extended arm.

Concentrate on maintaining speed and rhythm until the wall is touched.

Touch at full speed without slowing or altering stroke.

Take another stroke rather than overreaching for wall; overreaching disrupts rhythm and tends to make swimmer stop and glide into wall.

Develop ability to touch wall with either hand at any point in stroke.

Teaching Progression

A variety of simple activities can be used to help swimmers learn to finish effectively.

- Face forward and reach for wall from a stand (walk, drag, glide) without moving the head or other arm; this is simply to get youngsters used to reaching for and touching wall (other freestyle approaches, p. 132, can be used for this purpose).
- Face away from and reach for wall from a stand (walk, drag on heels, glide) without moving the head or other arm.
- Coordinate reach for wall with backstroke arm movements—stand, walk, drag, glide.
- Swim one (two, three, four) stroke(s) on back as if it were the last stroke in a race.
- Swim at a relaxed pace—on signal or when reaching a specified point in pool, sprint for wall; challenge swimmers to improve finish by timing sprint distances and recording and posting times.
- Have two or more youngsters practice finishing together; follow same sequence as outlined for individuals.
- Have two or more youngsters swim several (10, 15) strokes concentrating on the finish.
- Make sure youngsters practice touching at finish with either hand since they never know which arm will be back when they reach the wall.

Nonstop Rhythmical Aquatic Routines

Nonstop rhythmical aquatic routines involve 5, 10, 15, 30, or 45 minutes of continuous swimming activities. As youngsters build themselves up, gradually make practice sessions more challenging by repeating more active phases of routine two, three, or more times. Add variety by letting youngsters play such water games as follow the leader and add on where each swimmer repeats what those who went before did and adds a new activity. A simple routine might include:

- Kick across pool (and return).
- Use arms only in crossing pool (and return).
- Crawl stroke across pool (and return).
- Kick on back across pool (and return).
- Tread water using legs only for one (two) minute(s).
- Bob for one (two) minute(s).

- Crawl stroke length of pool (and return).
- Backstroke length of pool (and return).
- Crawl stroke length of pool (backstroke return).
- Backstroke length of pool (crawl stroke return).

Develop your own vigorous and progressively difficult routines by making new combinations, increasing repetitions, or swimming more and resting less. Emphasis in these routines is upon continuous activity for conditioning purposes rather than developing speed, improving form, or acquiring a sense of pace. However, this approach can be used to develop speed, improve form, and acquire a sense of pace. When active parts of routines are completed, ease out by floating and gliding.

Fun Activities

Swimming Games

Boys and girls love water games. Use this interest and the challenge of fun and competition to provide activities that will help youngsters develop speed, endurance, and better swimming skills.

There is no limit to the number and variety of games that can be used in water. Be creative and devise your own games according to interests, abilities, and needs of those you coach; encourage youngsters to create their own games and teach them to teammates. Select play activities with which youngsters are familiar so that the only new factors are the pool and water; introduce new games or play activities out of the pool. Many helpful games and related activities are described in *A Practical Guide for Teaching the Mentally Retarded to Swim,* (AAHPER: Washington, D.C., 1969).

Games described below represent only a small sample of those available. Specific games can be used to develop speed, endurance, or the concept of staying in lanes. To concentrate on a particular stroke—crawl or backstroke—limit action to that stroke; emphasize arm or leg action by confining activity to moving arms or kicking.

- *Chinese tag*—*It* chases and tries to tag other players. The person tagged becomes *It* and must hold the spot tagged while he chases others.
- *Plain tag*—*It* chases and tries to tag other players who swim away to avoid being tagged.
- *Underwater tag*—*It* chases and tries to tag other players when both are underwater. If *It* and the person being tagged are not underwater, then the same person remains *It*. *Variation:* A player is safe from being *It* if he is completely underwater.
- *Cross tag*—*It* designates another person whom he chases and tries to tag. If another person swims between the player being chased and *It*, he becomes the player to be chased.
- *Hill dill* (Pom pom pull away)—everyone but *It* lines up on one side of the pool. When *It* calls "hill dill" or "pom pom pull away" everyone tries to swim to the other side of the pool without being tagged or caught. Those tagged become helpers for *It* and help catch others—continue until all are caught.
- *Kitty in the water*—all players are in the water at the side of the pool; each player uses his spot as a base. *It* is in the middle of the pool and tries to tag players as they exchange places with each other. First (last) player tagged becomes *It*.
- *Follow the leader*—one player serves as leader and others follow him as he floats, dives, changes from back to front or front to back—change leaders every few minutes.
- *Bobbing race*—youngsters bob width (length, combinations) of the pool.
- *Kickboard race*—swimmers race width (length) of the pool using a kickboard.
- *Gliding race*—swimmers race width (length) of the pool using only arm strokes.
- *Crocodile race*—squad is divided into teams with an equal number of swimmers lined up behind each captain. Each participant places his hands on hips of swimmer in front of him. All except the first swimmer are confined to kicking action. Place youngster with strongest kick in back so as to keep line unbroken. *Variation:* Have each youngster lock his legs around waist of swimmer behind him so that each swimmer uses only his arms in a crawl stroke; only the last swimmer in each line kicks.
- *Obstacle race*—tubes, hoops, and other obstacles are put in the pool and swimmers are instructed to go under them, over them, or around them.
- *Neptune says*—this is an aquatic version of *Simon says*. It can be used to reinforce skills in swimming and diving and to keep youngsters alert—swimmers perform only when Neptune says to act. Use this game for particular dives, arm action, kicking, bobbing, and other activities.

Relays

Relays can be fun and provide youngsters with chances to cooperate and work together. They can also be used to teach basic concepts of formal relay competition. Include relays as one type of fun activity at the end of every practice session.

- *Crawl-backstroke relay*—teams of equal numbers line up on each side of pool. Backstrokers are in water on one side and crawl swimmers are on the deck. Action starts with crawl swimmers diving into water and swimming across pool; they touch the wall and their backstroke teammates take off. Continue as long as desired.
- *Crawl-backstroke medley relay*—each youngster swims across pool using crawl stroke and returns swimming backstroke. Repeat pattern twice (three or more times) before touching off teammates.
- *Crawl dive relay*—teams of equal numbers line up at side of pool. On *Go* one player from each team swims across pool and touches a teammate who swims across pool and touches a teammate who swims back. Have players

start on land to get practice in both diving and stroke.

Coaches can use a variety of relays to help youngsters develop speed, endurance, form, and swimming skills while having fun. Include two man relays, continuous relays for an odd number of swimmers, cross pool relays for an even number of swimmers, intrasquad relays and age medley relays (for details on these activities, see p. 134).

SUMMARY OF SPECIAL OLYMPICS SWIMMING RULES

25 and 50 Yard Freestyle

- Starting commands are: "Swimmers take your marks," followed by gun or whistle; starts are from deep end.
- Any stroke—even an unorthodox one—may be used.
- On turns in 50 yard freestyle, some part of swimmer's body must touch wall before he changes direction.
- A swimmer finishes when he touches end wall of pool.
- Standing on bottom is permitted but walking is not allowed and is cause for disqualification.
- Three false starts is cause for disqualification.

25 Yard Backstroke

- Start is in water with swimmer holding on to wall in accepted competitive manner; starts are from deep end.
- Starting commands are: "Swimmers take your marks," followed by gun or whistle.
- Any stroke—even an unorthodox one—may be used providing swimmer is on his back at all times.
- Three false starts is cause for disqualification.
- Standing on bottom is permitted but walking is not allowed and is cause for disqualification.
- Swimmer must still be on his back when he touches wall at finish.

100 Yard Freestyle Relay

- Lead off man starts from a standing position on deck unless he elects to start in water holding on to wall, in which case, he pushes off at sound of gun.
- Second, third, and fourth swimmers enter water from a sitting or standing position on edge of pool after any part of incoming swimmer's body has touched wall.
- Standing on bottom is permitted but any member of a relay team who walks causes his team to be disqualified.
- A team is disqualified if any member of the team starts before his incoming teammate has touched wall.
- Three false starts by lead-off man disqualifies his team.
- A team finishes when its anchor man touches wall to complete his leg.

SELECTED SWIMMING REFERENCES

American Association for Health, Physical Education and Recreation. *A Practical Guide for Teaching the Mentally Retarded to Swim.* Washington, D.C.: The Association (1201 16th St., N.W.), 1969.

American National Red Cross. *Teaching Johnny to Swim.* Washington, D.C.: American National Red Cross, 1963.

Athletic Institute. *How to Improve Your Swimming.* Chicago, Illinois: The Institute (805 Merchandise Mart). (Filmstrip with same title complements publication.)

Braaten, J. and Lea, I. *Swimming Program for the Trainable Retarded: Guide I, II, and III.* Toronto, Ontario, Canada: Canadian Association for Retarded Children (87 Bedford Road).

Brown, Richard L. and Moriarty, Phil. *Swimming.* New Brunswick, New Jersey: Boy Scouts of America, 1963.

Gabrielsen, M. Alexander, Spears, Betty, and Gabrielsen, B. W. *Aquatics Handbook (Second Edition).* Englewood Cliffs, New Jersey: Prentice-Hall, Inc., 1968.

Grosse, Susan J. Annotated Bibliography: *Swimming for the Handicapped* (Mimeographed). Washington, D.C.: American Association for Health, Physical Education, and Recreation (1201 16th St., N.W.), 1969.

Weiser, Ron (Editor). *Swimming Manual.* Pomona, California: Pacific State Hospital (Rehabilitation Services Department, Box 100).

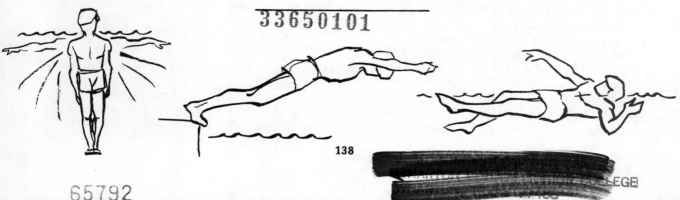